BLACK ROBE
FEVER

Bryan & Whitlock
Hope you enjoy!

2/16

BLACK ROBE FEVER

BY GARY L. RICHARDSON

6450 S. LEWIS, SUITE 300
TULSA, OK 74136
(918) 492-7674

TATE PUBLISHING
AND ENTERPRISES, LLC

Four things belong to a judge:
to hear courteously,
to answer wisely,
to consider soberly, and
to decide impartially.

— Socrates

Published by Tate Publishing & Enterprises, LLC
127 E. Trade Center Terrace | Mustang, Oklahoma 73064 USA
1.888.361.9473 | www.tatepublishing.com

Tate Publishing is committed to excellence in the publishing industry. The company reflects the philosophy established by the founders, based on Psalm 68:11,
"The Lord gave the word and great was the company of those who published it."

Published in the United States of America

ISBN: 978-1-68118-707-5
1. Biography & Autobiography / General
2. Biography & Autobiography / Lawyers & Judges
15.10.21

If American justice means anything at all,
it stands for the equitable administration of the law
toward every citizen and resident of the United States.
Under our constitutional system of jurisprudence,
each individual in this country has the right
to be treated equally by the legal process,
and should any person ever have to appear in court,
whether for civil or criminal reasons,
he or she is entitled to expect
a fair and impartial trial.

DEDICATION

I dedicate this book to my deceased father,
my hero,
who helped me learn about fear,
which is covered in my book,
Fear Is Never Your Friend, and
who helped me learn
that all bullies are "cowards",
even the bullies wearing the black robes.

PREFACE

As a young, passionate attorney, the statement above was my fervent belief. I had gone to law school to become a servant of the people. I wanted to serve all people, but I had the biggest heart for the ones the world refers to as "the *little* people," the people with *little* power, *little* hope, and *little* clout. Ensuring that each person's rights are protected is an enormous responsibility, and in our American justice system, this responsibility falls primarily upon attorneys and judges. If and when deviations from legitimate procedures occur, especially in the courts, they diminish our cherished rule of law. Fortunately, given the thousands of cases that are adjudicated each year, such breakdowns are relatively rare. However, they do take place, and when they do, real people are hurt.

Since childhood, I had considered the legal profession to be one of the highest callings one could aspire to, and believed that judges were members of an objective and esteemed fraternity at the very top. I was shocked the first time, as a new lawyer, idealistic and naive, I encountered a judge infected with Black Robe Fever. To my great dismay, I discovered there are some black-robed autocrats that disdain the individuals who appear before them. There are others who are mentally impaired or simply incompetent, and there are a few that are unquestionably crooked. I have witnessed judges who cursed like drunken sailors from the bench, dispatched defendants to mental institutions without granting them their constitutional right to a hearing, and, during one incident, mimicked a chicken to chide and ridicule another attorney. This occurred early in my career. I told myself that, surely, his bizarre behavior was an aberration.

Much to my disappointment, the longer I practiced law, the more widespread I found this type of epidemic to be. I've since encountered judges who showed obvious and relentless prejudice, many who were openly hostile to witnesses or who improperly attempted to influence juries, and, on one notable occasion, I faced an intoxicated jurist who was in no condition to perform his duties. I've met judges who didn't care if anyone got his or her fair day in court and judges who dictated to lawyers precisely how they were to present their cases. In short, I soon realized that Black Robe Fever was real, unchecked, and accelerating.

This book was not necessarily written as a call to action, but instead as a call to awaken-a call to awaken to the dangers of a fever that has the power to jeopardize the integrity of one of our most precious cornerstones of freedom, our judicial system. This fever, *black robe fever,* behaves like a virus, seriously weakening the very system we rely on for the foundation of what is good and right about our country. Our Judges are not only entrusted with a great responsibility to uphold the law, they take office and swear to do so. They tell those who vote for them that they will do so. It is an awesome responsibility and we often need them to protect us from ourselves and yet, as you will learn through the stories in this book, sometimes we need to be protected from our protectors.

It has been my sad experience that most lawyers do not, and will not, stand up against abusive Judges (the cowards) even at the expense of their clients' loss at the hands of, again, abusive Judges. Too many attorneys fear the significant consequences of taking a stand against an out of control judge. Even if they wanted to, many attorneys, especially the younger ones, do not know how to go about protecting their clients' rights under these circumstances. For me, I never saw it as much, taking *a stand against* what was wrong, as I did, taking *a stand for* what was right. I have lived my life determined to do all I can to protect people from being abused by a system designed to protect them. And in the end, my desire to see justice done was greater than my fear of any personal consequence.

Beginning with my career as an assistant district attorney in 1974, this book presents a collection of my most memorable encounters with unrestrained, disgraceful judges, and abusive law enforcement officials. I hope "Black Robe Fever" will help you understand that some judges, as well as others in the judicial system, are dangerous impediments to a fair trial and what they do is an egregious breach of the pubic trust.

This is America, the land of the free. Any time we wish; we can open a book that will open our minds to new information, understanding, and knowledge. My hope is that reading this book will be one of those times for you. I anticipate that the true stories I share will shock, fascinate and intrigue you, and that this book will give you a new and broader perspective from which to view our judicial system. Unless and until those infected by Black Robe

Fever are held accountable and removed from office or positions of influence, justice for all will be simply a promise America cannot keep.

Gary L. Richardson
Tulsa, Oklahoma
Spring, 2002

As a trial lawyer
if you aren't willing to risk
your own freedom
to protect your client's rights
when necessary,
then consider
getting out of the business.
As you read *Black Robe Fever,*
you will see why the author says this.

One thing I have learned thru the years about "cowards" is that by in large they all seek positions of POWER as the more power a coward receives the SAFE the coward feels. And once a coward gets power the coward will become a bully. So, when dealing with a judge or anyone else and they are being a bully we know we are dealing with a "coward". One exception to this rule is that sometimes a person that is in a tough profession, such as being a trial lawyer, and is being a bully it could be that this person is attempting to conceal a kind heart that he/she doesn't want revealed.

- Gary Richardson

TABLE OF CONTENTS

CHAPTER 1

CARTER'S LAW

Trial and Errors in a Sick Man's Courtroom

"You're a g*ddamn little chickensh*t!" Judge John W. Carter, Jr. shrieked at the tearful young man who stood before him. The young man was accused of breaking into a high school in a nearby town and stealing audio equipment. "What a son-of-a-b*tch," the sixty-three-year-old jurist added under his breath for good measure.

I couldn't believe my ears. Nothing in law school had prepared me for such verbal abuse of a defendant by a judge. During the twelve months I'd been an assistant district attorney in Muskogee, Oklahoma, I thought I'd heard the worst that John Carter could dispense, but this blasphemous outburst was grotesque. This day's outburst went to a new level. I grabbed the armrest of my chair and started to stand up to object. Judge Carter saw the look of disgust on my face. He angrily gestured for me to remain seated ... and quiet.

Police had stopped the boy and three of his friends shortly after they drove away from Ft. Gibson High School, headed for a Muskogee pawn shop a few miles down the highway. Today, surrounded by his mother, the other boys and their parents, the school principal, and a deputy sheriff, the nervous young man sobbed and confessed to being the driver of the getaway car, but he denied knowing that the equipment was stolen. At least, he hadn't realized it until just before they were arrested. The boy tried to invoke a religious angle - the judge was reputed to go lightly on believers - by pleading that he needed to get this proceeding over with as quickly as possible so he could depart on a weekend outing with his church group.

Judge Carter sighed and began to speak calmly. "Son, when you learned the equipment was stolen ..." His voiced trailed off. Then he jerked bolt upright in his chair and stabbed his finger toward one of the other boys. He screamed. "Why didn't you tell that little son-of-a-bitch to f- himself and get out of your car and walk?"

The room was silent as a tomb. I leapt from my chair, and my brain raced for words to match my outrage. The judge glared at me, daring me to open my mouth. For nearly half a minute, I stared back without saying anything. Carter was a judge out of control, a sick man, and a threat to the American judicial system. Unfortunately, he wasn't one of a kind. I knew instinctively that this judge must be dealt with, but not now and not here. For this battle, I knew I needed help, help from someone that had more power and authority than I did.

Muskogee is a nondescript community of 40,000 hardy and churchgoing folks in the eastern Oklahoma foothills of the Ozarks. Singer Merle Haggard lent it a bit of toe-tapping notoriety with his Sixties' ballad, "Okie From Muskogee," but the city was once better known as a favorite playground and hiding place for some of the Old West's more colorful bandits. In fact, Muskogee remained a legend among Oklahoma lawmen for more than a century after its rough beginnings in 1872 where routes of the Missouri, Kansas, and Texas Railroad merged. Several locals swear little has changed, with outlaw's ghosts still haunting the area.

I had heard stories regarding this "untamed" settlement for years, but I didn't pay much attention until I was offered a job as an assistant district attorney for Muskogee County. It was late 1974, and I lived in Oklahoma City where I had served for a year as Oklahoma's assistant insurance commissioner. When the opportunity came, I was eighteen months out of law school and excited to get into the courtroom. Nonetheless, I was wary enough to check out some of the tales I'd heard about "Muskogee justice" before moving my family from the secure predictability of the state capital to what sounded like the ragged edges of the frontier. Even though my wife was a native of Muskogee, our new hometown-to-be, and looked forward to the transfer, members of the Oklahoma Bureau of Investigation and numerous people in the judicial system, including several in the criminal division of the state's attorney general's office, repeatedly warned me that Muskogee was the most corrupt place in Oklahoma.

Most new lawyers would probably have passed up the chance to launch their careers in an area with such a reputation, but I've always liked a challenge - the bigger, the better. So in January of 1975, one month shy of my thirty-third birthday, I joined Julian Fite's staff, the recently elected Muskogee County district attorney. Already on board were three experienced assistant D.A.s who knew their way around the courthouse, maybe the hazards of this intriguing locale had been overstated.

My first assignment was the juvenile division, and my office, like the others, was a cubicle hardly big enough to turn around in. I hadn't been on the job long, not more than a couple of days when I was first exposed to what I have since dubbed Black Robe Fever.

My new compatriots had not explained Judge John W. Carter Jr. to me, except for occasional whispers about the man's erratic behavior.

"You won't believe this wacko," one assistant D.A. asserted. Another cautioned that it would be, "Katie, bar the door if you *tick*[1] him off." I was about to learn that their opinions were understatements at best.

Carter was the county's associate district judge, a position he had held since 1969. I remember our first meeting, a curt handshake — in silence. He was about five-feet ten-inches tall, his dark-complexion matched his black hair. A nice-looking older man, I concluded at the time. But, as they say, looks can be deceiving.

The judge was a native of Eufaula, Oklahoma, a tiny settlement thirty-five miles to the south as the buzzard flies, and he had lived in Muskogee for forty years. In 1935, right out of law school, Carter had set up private practice in the city. Before he assumed his present position, he had served as a police judge, assistant county attorney, and a county judge. Because of his widely reported "colorful" courtroom style, most everybody in town knew of him. Since he handled probate and juvenile issues, and I was in charge of juvenile matters for the D.A.'s office, my cases went to him. From day one, my appearances before the judge constituted a psychological roller coaster. For a new attorney and prosecutor, it was truly a baptism by fire.

###

---

[1] My word-it is easy to guess the word used in the original quote.

Carter's antics were unpredictable. Some days — even weeks — he was, as the old expression goes, sober as a judge. Other times, his conduct ranged from inane to insane. One of my initial encounters involved the son of an amiable couple I knew from my church. Their shy boy stood next to his parents in Carter's austere courtroom and waited for the judge's decision. What happened next was such an affront to civilized decorum that I've forgotten the reason the young man had been brought in.

"If you cared a whit about this little son-of-a-b*tch of yours," he yelled at the couple in open court, "I wouldn't have to be wasting my time today." The man and woman lowered their heads: embarrassed and ashamed. Carter kept going.

"Your juvenile delinquent wouldn't be here if you were real parents!" He stabbed his index finger toward the woman. "Especially you, lady." When the couple left the courtroom with their son, all three were crying.

Judge Carter erupted in another scurrilous outburst in a case involving the commitment of a juvenile to a mental hospital. Michael Kelly, the client's lawyer and a respected member of the community, politely questioned the judge's reasoning on a particular point. Carter shook his fist and screamed, "Don't challenge me, Mister Big Shot! You're not going to win this case, no matter what you do."

Kelly frowned at the tirade.

Carter jumped up, tapped his chin, and dared the attorney to hit him. "Go ahead, you son of a b*tch, duke me!"

Kelly refused to rise to the bait.

Carter laughed and called him a chicken, then followed the attorney out of the courtroom, flapping his arms and clucking, "chickensh*t, chickensh*t, that's what you are!"

A few days later, an elderly man respectfully petitioned the judge to commit his ailing wife to Eastern State Hospital at Vinita, one of Oklahoma's mental facilities. Carter was notorious for perfunctorily signing such orders without a formal hearing. After a few minutes of idle conversation with the man, the judge agreed to commit the woman. To the astonishment of everyone in the courtroom, Carter shipped the husband away also.

I'll never forget the afternoon I was sitting in my office when my secretary buzzed the intercom. It was 2:15 p.m.

"Mr. Richardson, Judge Carter's out here with another gentleman and a welfare worker, and he's really upset and wants to talk to you." I took a deep breath and replied, "Please send him in."

Carter huffed into my office and positioned himself in front of my desk. With him was the father of the young man he was there to discuss and a welfare worker who was a friend of mine. Carter leaned forward, placed his palms on my desk, and yelled in my face.

"Where the hell were you? We had a hearing scheduled for two o'clock in my chambers!"

I ran my finger down the open page of my daily calendar then shook my head. "I'm sorry, your honor, but I didn't know about it. It's not on my calendar."

Carter rolled his eyes and started yelling again. I casually reached over and tapped the intercom. My secretary confirmed that there was nothing of this matter on her calendar either. I looked at Carter and smiled serenely.

"Well, judge," I said, "If there's a hearing, I guess we'd better go upstairs and have it."

My associates frequently told me my congenial response under fire was evidence of my orneriness. I disagree. It was my way of maintaining my equal role as an officer of the court. But I wasn't quite finished with this exchange.

Carter had apoplexy whenever anyone entered his courtroom with a Coke or similar refreshment in hand. Just before we left my office, I purposely stopped at the coffee unit and poured myself a full cup. The judge glared at me, incensed at my flagrant disregard for his hidebound procedures. As we started up the stairwell, he quickly moved to within a few inches of my heels and continued his nagging.

"Damn it, Richardson, why? I mean, just *why?*" His shrill voice resembled the yapping of a Chihuahua, and echoed down the narrow, marble passageway.

"I want an answer out of you! Why weren't you in my courtroom when you were suppose to have been? You hear me, Richardson?"

I chose not to reply.

Even though Judge Carter's courtroom was not in session at the time, when I entered the empty courtroom with my cup of coffee, Carter pointed his finger at the offending beverage and screamed, "You get the hell out of here with that!" I nodded politely and walked toward the hall. The welfare worker scurried to follow me to safety. The judge seized the boy's father and pulled him inside the courtroom. Before the door closed, he yelled at me again.

"Damn it, Richardson, I want an answer from you! Why weren't you in my courtroom at two?"

I turned and replied with a sigh. "Judge, I'd be more than happy to give you an answer, but I know you really don't want an answer. You just want to holler at me."

Carter gritted his teeth, as he began mocking my response in a singsong manner. "You really don't want an answer; you really don't want an answer." He slammed the courtroom door.

My welfare friend and I discussed several matters while I finished my coffee. When we stepped into the outer area of the judge's chambers, we were talking about something humorous which had nothing at all to do with Carter's hearing. We laughed briefly at the conclusion of our story. It was too much for the judge. He grabbed the young man's dad, pointed at me, and bellowed, "I want you to look at him. Laughing at a time like this! What kind of a father could ever raise a son like that?"

Carter's words were an indirect attack not lost on the father of the juvenile.

Almost immediately, the hallway door opened, and the sheriff brought in the young man who was the subject of the hearing. All of us went into the judge's chambers. Carter sat down and calmly proceeded to conduct the session as if nothing had happened. It was an incredible performance. I peered at his expressionless face and I genuinely had to wonder if he had Alzheimer's.

Had I imagined the past 30 minutes?

Did I have Alzheimer's?

The "last straw" which convinced me that immediate and drastic action had to be taken was Carter's courtroom outburst against the boy who had driven the getaway car from the high school break-in, which I related at the beginning of the chapter. That outrageous spectacle, which occurred in March of 1975, left me shaken and totally committed to pursue the judge's removal from office, however long it might take and regardless of the personal consequences.

I'll never forget the tears in the eyes of the boy's mother who stood mute beside her sobbing son. Without question, the young man had broken the law, but Judge Carter ignored his contrite attitude and preceded to strip away his remaining self-respect with the most foul and demeaning language I had ever heard in a public forum.

Immediately after that shocking performance, I sprinted downstairs to my boss's office, Julian Fite.

"Something has to be done about Carter," I pleaded with Fite. "Now"

I had complained to the district attorney before, but the judge's earlier performances paled in comparison.

"No human being should have to put up with that kind of abuse," I nearly shouted.

The D.A. sat motionless for a moment. Finally, he replied with a quiet, "Yeah, I know."

That wasn't good enough for me. Within minutes, I was on the phone with Marian P. Opala, the state courts administrator in Oklahoma City. I told him what this arrogant, malicious, and sick judge was doing and that the man had to be stopped. I stressed that no one in the Muskogee D.A. 's office wanted to deal with Carter, for fear of retribution.

"Whenever anything is scheduled before Judge Carter that my co-workers suspect might trigger threats against any of us," I explained, "they send me upstairs to his courtroom. Fearing what he might do, they don't want to take him on, under any circumstances. And that includes the office staff."

Opala asked how I conducted myself in front of the judge. In others words, what was my key to survival?

"I never argue with him," I answered without hesitation. "I never interact with his foolishness. I just stand there and endure the ranting and raving. When he finishes, I try to respond coolly and professionally." I took a deep breath. "Maintaining my composure always seems to disarm him."

After nearly a half-hour of aggressive questioning about particular cases and Carter's accompanying exhibitions, Opala agreed to come to Muskogee.

"But," he commented, "I'll have to make certain arrangements first."

"How long will *that* take?" My voice reflected my exasperation.

"I'll be there within 30 days," Opala promised. He assured me it was the best he could do.

The next afternoon, as I walked past the door to Judge Carter's chambers, I overheard him bragging to an attorney who was attempting to argue a legal point.

"I don't care what those clowns decide the law is over there in Oklahoma City. The law in this courtroom is Carter's Law!"

Fortunately, Carter's perversion of "law" was about to change.

I had left the district attorney's office for private practice only a few days before States Courts Administrator, Marian P. Opala, drove the one-hundred-and-thirty-eight miles from Oklahoma City to Muskogee, but I remained available and prepared to do whatever was necessary to terminate the tyrannical reign of Judge John W. Carter, Jr.

It was April, 1975. Opala came to town without fanfare, and he conducted his hearing in an equally low-key manner. The meeting was informal, and open only to Carter and those who had faced his courtroom antics. A formal investigation, if there were to be one, would come later.

Two dozen people attended that session, including me. I listened as parents, attorneys, a minister, and a line-up of others recounted the sordid events: Judge Carter's abusive and improper language from the bench, his cursing of their children and clients, the frequent denial of defendant's constitutional rights, and, in some instances, his refusal to allow defense lawyers the opportunity to present their side of a case. One attorney charged that the judge's conduct was the most flagrant mockery of justice one could imagine. Many of those present sadly agreed with him.

During the hearing, Opala interviewed individuals both singularly and in groups, but all who attended received the time necessary to relate, in detail, the harms inflicted by Carter. Seven of those who met with him said they would file accusations about the judge with the state Council on Judicial Complaints, and Opala promised to mail the appropriate forms to them. Later, when he was approached by reporters and asked about the hearing, Opala said only that it had taken place. He refused to describe the nature of the complaints or to reveal the names of the complainants.

Earlier that month, presiding District Judge William H. Haworth Jr. had relieved Carter of some of his duties in dealing with juveniles. That action was taken immediately after Carter had called Haworth "a poor example for juveniles when you are being investigated yourself."

Carter's quip wasn't just a cheap shot. The Council on Judicial Complaints had indeed begun an investigation on Haworth's conduct at the beginning of the year.

"Muskogee justice," it appeared, was finally attracting attention it richly deserved.

At the time he sidelined Carter, Judge Haworth said it resulted from a meeting he'd had with representatives of city, county, and state agencies, following numerous complaints that juveniles were being denied their constitutional rights. Haworth determined that there had been instances of "lie detector tests being administered to children from 6 to 18 years of age without advice of counsel and, in certain instances, without their parents being present." Judge Haworth also said he had invited Carter to the meeting but that the associate judge "used profanity" and refused to attend. Haworth told Carter he would not tolerate such abuse. The threat fell on deaf ears. Shortly thereafter, Carter launched a letter-writing campaign to various politicians, heads of bar groups, and newspapers to air his criticisms of justice in Muskogee County in general and of Haworth in particular. It was a classic case of the pot calling the kettle black.

But Judge Carter's belligerent days were winding down. On April 29, 1975, the *Muskogee Daily Phoenix* headlined, "Carter to take 30-Day Leave From Duties."

The first paragraph of the front-page story read, "Associate District Judge John Carter Jr., recently the subject of complaints from a group of parents and attorneys who have appeared before him, notified District Judge Bill Haworth Monday that he intends to take a thirty-day leave from his job." In the article, Carter apologized for any behavior that might have caused offense.

Reporters wanted Marian Opala's reaction to Carter's sudden decision, but his only comment was that he had discussed the complaints with Ben T. Williams, chief justice of the Oklahoma Supreme Court.

Three months later, on August 6, Judge Carter publicly confirmed that he was the subject of an investigation by the Council on Judicial Complaints for alleged misconduct in office. He admitted he had been served a subpoena by an agent of the Oklahoma State Bureau of Investigation to appear before the three-member council on August 9 at the state Bar Center in Oklahoma City.

"I'm bound to have lost my temper a time or two," he offered simply. I don't think that justifies ouster."

The formal investigation began right after lunch on a steamy Saturday. Bumper-to-bumper witnesses reiterated the abuses suffered and reinforced the image of a sick man who had no business sitting on the bench. Carter countered with partial explanations and apologies, and a physician offered medical rationalizations for the judge's sometimes-erratic behavior. But, virtually from the beginning, the outcome was evident. Unfortunately for the residents of Muskogee County, the formal step — Carter's removal-was to be months away. Not surprisingly, judges are protective of their own, and the Council on Judicial Complaints wanted to be certain that Carter "deserved" what would amount to a humiliating termination of his career.

While the Council deliberated Carter's fate, it decided that of his boss. In November of 1975, District Judge William Haworth, was tossed out of office for "corruption, oppression, and improper political activity." In addition, Haworth was accused of running a loan operation in his chambers, and he was banned from ever holding public office ever again. Ironically, with Haworth out of the way, Carter became the highest-ranking judge in a county desperate for honest administration of the law.

Looking back on Judge Haworth and his reign, I didn't have many direct dealings with him while I was an assistant district attorney in Muskogee, although I did know that some in eastern Oklahoma had long considered him a crook. Even so, Haworth was often so comical he was almost likable. It was frequently said that he would rather climb a tree to tell a lie than stand on the ground and tell the truth.

As far as procedures went, Haworth was a fairly good judge, but he couldn't resist temptation. He was in his fifties and a very smart politico whose trick was to get someone obligated to him. Setting people up, was his perpetual game. One day, he approached me in the hall and asked how things were going right after I had gone into private practice. "Slow," I answered honestly. "It's a little tough getting started."

He smiled. "I figured it might be. I've got some friends who have a real good lawsuit, if you know what I mean. I'm gonna have them give you a call."

"In that case, judge," I replied, "I'm real busy."

"No, I'm serious," he insisted with a sly smile.

I shook my head. "I'm serious, too."

I went to see Special Judge Jay Cook, Haworth's protégé, and I told him, "You need to tell Judge Haworth that he can't buy me, so he might as well quit trying. "I'm not for sale."

On March 23, 1976, twelve months after I first called Opala, Judge Carter announced that he would resign, ending a thirteen-year career on the Muskogee County bench. He cited "physical disabilities." Curiously, Carter's decision *to resign* followed a petition filed with the Court of the Judiciary by Chief Justice Ben T. Williams of the Oklahoma Supreme Court just twenty-four hours previously, that called for the judge's forced retirement.

Carter told the media he'd known all along about the William's petition, interestingly, reported to be the first of it's kind in Oklahoma history. As a matter of fact, he asserted, the two men had even planned the maneuver together.

"Well, I just couldn't write in and quit, telling them I just feel bad," Carter declared. "We did this so it wouldn't appear I was milking the pension fund."

Carter said he would travel to Oklahoma City, accompanied by his wife, attorney, and doctor, and inform the Judiciary Court under oath that he agreed with the petition, which specified that he receive retirement compensation.

"I guess I insulted my friends and got loose with my language and flew off the handle," the judge asserted. "My wife had told me things I said that shocked me. I didn't remember saying them."

Carter stated that during the last five years he had been plagued by cancer and hypertension and his doctor had advised him the previous year that his medical problems were getting worse and that he should step down.

"I wanted to go out with my boots on," he added, "but my wife and doctor convinced me to retire. They didn't want to see me kill myself at this job."

But the deplorable affair wasn't over yet. Three days later, Carter reneged, saying he would remain in office for at least several more months while the Court on judiciary prepared for its initial hearing on his physical competency. The trial date on his forced retirement was set for June 15.

"The longer I stay here the better off I am," Carter quipped. "I hope they forget the whole thing." Carter would reach his legal retirement age in November, and he knew that each day he remained in office meant a heftier pension.

"Carter's Law" finally ended on June 15, 1976, when Oklahoma's Court of the Judiciary forced him from office. A month earlier, the judge had voluntarily suspended himself. He'd already indicated he did not intend to fight the ouster charges.

Characteristically, during one of his last judicial acts, Carter caused a stir by railing at two black parents accused of child abuse. "It's people like you who ruin your race. I know animals that live better than you people." Carter signed an order turning over custody of their child to the Welfare Department and bolted from the courtroom, slamming the door behind him.

But at mid-afternoon on Tuesday, June 15, after hours of disastrous testimony from witnesses for the prosecution, tempered by benign medical reports that Carter's "irrational behavior" might have been caused by the lengthy list of ailments and medications, the Court on the Judiciary ordered Carter retired from office on the grounds of physical disability. The nine judges mandated that Carter be compulsorily retired effective June 30 and that his earlier suspension from office continue until that time. The court granted Carter full retirement compensation, which, based on his salary and years of service, was $906.25 per month-a lifetime pension of $10,875 per year (remember, those were 1976 dollars).

###

Much has changed in Muskogee, Oklahoma, since those days. Its citizens now have the good jurists they deserve. Haworth and Carter are gone. Judge Jay Cook, another Muskogee Judge, who was dispatched to the state penitentiary for taking traffic ticket money, followed them in short order.

Of the three, perhaps Carter was the most honest. I even intimated that at the formal hearing when his lawyer asked me, "Mr. Richardson, are you stating that Judge Carter is a dishonest man?"

"No, sir," I replied, "and that's the sad part about all this. God only knows we need honest judges in Muskogee. Judge Carter, in my opinion, is a sick man, but he's not dishonest."

Before the official proceedings ended, several others, including district attorney Julian Fite, repeated my sentiments.

Regardless of what he had done, when John W. Carter Jr. left the hearing, defeated and in disgrace, I genuinely felt sorry for him. In his own way, he may have been a forthright, hard-working, and dedicated jurist, and I'm sure he believed that he was. But, because of his profound disabilities, Judge Carter was not fit to sit in judgment of his fellow man- and hadn't been for years. The real tragedy was that it took so long for the system to acknowledge the problem and take the necessary steps to protect the public.

###

One afternoon, not long after Judge Carter retired, I was leaving the Muskogee post office and encountered Judge Carter. I saw him strutting toward me, and with no way to avoid him I smiled as he approached.

"You!" he pointed at me and yelled. "I'm going to get you if it's the last thing I do." I waited until he came alongside, and reached to put my arm around him.

"Now, judge," I declared in a calm voice, "You can't mean that. Someday you might even thank me for saving your health. As a matter of fact, you might even give me a cut of your generous pension," I said in humor.

I can't be sure, but I thought I caught the beginning of a grin.

CHAPTER 2

THE WRIGHT MOVES
— TO JAIL

Fifty-one Strikes and You're Out!

While I was still a new assistant district attorney in Muskogee, I handled a case that no one else in our office wanted to touch, much less bring to trial. "A dud," "too difficult," and "a no-winner," were just a few of their more generous assessments. The real reason was that the victim of the crime was the uncle of our district attorney, Julian Fite. The other prosecutors, as well as the police who'd investigated the crime, feared that failure to convict under such delicate circumstances might have negative repercussions on their careers. Better to let sleeping dogs lie, they'd prudently concluded.

Doctor Fite, the D.A.'s uncle, was a prominent local physician whose residence had been burglarized of thousands of dollars in silverware, jewelry, and other valuables. Donald Lee Wright, the alleged perpetrator, was arrested shortly after the break-in. This guy was an interesting individual. "Unique" might be a better word to describe his many uncommon characteristics.

Wright in his mid-thirties was handsome, confident, and gregarious. He looked like a prosperous bank executive, and he dressed and carried himself like one. However, he had never had, to our knowledge, full-time employment. Yet he lived with his pretty blond wife and their new baby in an attractive two-story home in Tahlequah, a community east of Muskogee, always drove new cars, and had numerous other expensive tastes. He traveled across the country to ply his "business," flying first class and staying in the best hotels. But his chutzpah was what really set him apart. When he was arrested, he was playing shortstop on the Tahlequah police department's softball team.

Wright was taken into custody and charged with burglary before Julian Fite was elected to office as Muskogee County district attorney. There had been little interest in pursuing Wright's prosecution at the time of the arrest because of the difficulty of the case and the fact that the case largely depended on Wright's nephew's testimony. All that changed after Fite came on the scene. The case had been passed on the docket for at least two years and, as the saying goes, it was "getting hair on it." Not surprisingly, because of the family relationship, the newly elected D .A. emphasized to us that he wanted a trial. Period, win or lose.

Once someone is charged with a crime, the concept of a "speedy trial" comes into play. However, if the defendant doesn't request quick action, the matter can stay on the books for years, as this one had. For obvious reasons, criminal defendants usually don't insist on going to trial, and Father Time can be their most important ally. Wright was no exception. He was out on bond, and he was perfectly satisfied with the status quo.

When Julian Fite ordered a trial for Wright, it wasn't exactly the most thrilling news my fellow prosecutors wanted to hear, and everyone wondered who would get the unpleasant assignment. A day later, Fite selected his chief assistant who was an experienced trial attorney. There were sighs of relief among the others in the office. At this point I had quickly established a reputation by winning several tough cases and had a fourteen case winning streak, which was reported as a record for our county. A few months after selecting his chief assistant, Fite called me into his office.

"I've changed my mind. Donald Wright is yours. I want you to prosecute the case."

I was both surprised and pleased. Fite's decision meant that I had arrived. His number-one man was indeed a master supervisor, and he was loyal to his boss, but I knew I had that "fire in the belly" which was going to be needed if Wright were going to get what he deserved - jail. As I now had some successful courtroom experience under my belt, I gladly accepted the challenge. The parameters were unambiguous: The case was Fite's personal cause. The crook needed to be convicted, and, most importantly, I genuinely believed I could put this guy behind bars.

Wright had the proverbial arms-length rap sheet, with some thirty charges on it. However, even though he had been tried a few times, he had never been convicted on any of them. We knew he was, at best, a thief, and a first class one at that, and it was time for him to go to jail. We immediately set the case for trial.

This was to be my first appearance before Judge Billy Jack Jackson (not his real name), a laid-back, country-type from a small Oklahoma town just east of Muskogee. The man in the black robe was in his late thirties or early forties, and he stood two inches shy of six feet. "Billy Jack" as his friends called him, was a roving judge who occasionally traveled to Muskogee to hold court. I had heard a tale about him that piqued my curiosity: Billy Jack supposedly had a habit of telling attorneys how to do their business. I hoped this was just a rumor. When I went upstairs to the courtroom on the first morning of the trial, I found out otherwise.

My prosecution strategy was in place, the witnesses were ready, and I walked into the courtroom full of confidence. Sam Caldwell, Donald Wright's attorney was already seated and was making copious notes on a legal pad. Caldwell, then in his sixties, was considered one of the top defense lawyers in eastern Oklahoma. As I started to sit down, Judge Jackson motioned for Caldwell and me to follow him into his chambers. I frowned. It was unusual to start a trial this way.

Once the door closed, Jackson put his hands on his hips and smiled at me.

"Mr. Richardson," he began, "I've read the transcript of the preliminary hearing, and there's no way you can win this case. So, I've talked to Mr. Caldwell, and he's agreed to plead out Mr. Wright to a misdemeanor. I want you to reduce the charges, accept his plea, and I'm going to give him six months to a year in county jail.

For a second, I thought I hadn't heard him correctly.

"You want me to do *what?*"

"Misdemeanor, counselor, and that's that."

I was shocked. I'd read the same transcript. I knew that the answer he wanted to his question was "Yes." I also knew a conviction was a long shot, but I wanted the opportunity. Even though I wasn't sure I could convict Wright, I believed that it was wrong that the man had lived such a life of crime and been tried and acquitted so many times. Surely this would be the good guys' time.

I shook my head. "Judge, I'm sorry, but my answer is No. I can't do what you are asking. This man needs to be convicted of a felony."

Judge Jackson squinted at me. "You don't understand, Mr. Richardson. I told you that's what I want you to do."

I stood my ground, and once again calmly answered, "No, sir." Maybe he thought he could take advantage of me because I was young, with a short time as a prosecutor, but I believed in what I was doing, and couldn't find another answer in me but, "No."

"I can't honor your request, Your Honor, I won't. Donald Wright has a laundry list of charges he's never been convicted of. There are at least thirty that we know of. There have even been a few trials on some of them, but he has been acquitted every time." I looked straight into his eyes. "You may be right that we can't win this case, but the state has the right to try it. Respectfully sir, my answer must be, 'No.'"

The judge was furious. His face grew red, and his mouth tightened. He was not used to having a lawyer tell him "No", even when he was outside his authority as a judge. Without saying anything, he headed for the courtroom. Caldwell and I followed, and the trial began.

We weren't thirty minutes into the proceedings before Judge Jackson began giving me bad rulings — repeatedly sustaining Caldwell's objections, giving him rulings he was not entitled to. At first, since I never tried a case before Jackson, I thought that he might have a hearing problem. On the other hand, maybe he wasn't well versed in the legal grounds for objections. But his one-sided decisions continued, and they were so obviously wrong that longtime observers in the courtroom coughed and squirmed. I chafed at Jackson's intentional acts of revenge, but I attempted to stay with my game plan.

At one point, I walked toward the chalkboard to illustrate a fact. By this time, I had decided to go beyond my boundaries as a lawyer, something for which I could suffer consequences, but by now, I had made a conscious decision to suffer whatever consequences my conduct brought, in view of the gross injustice that the judge was rendering. Caldwell objected even before I could write the pertinent information I wanted to present to the jury, and Judge Jackson sustained him, denying me the right to do something during trial that is time and again allowed in the process of trying a case. I glared at the judge, but it made no difference. A few minutes later, I asked a question of a witness which, if answered honestly, would have been devastating to the defense. Before the witness could answer, Caldwell quickly jumped to his feet and objected by shaking his head. Judge Jackson asked him what the grounds were.

"It's, uh-uh-uh, repetitious, your honor."

"Sustained!" Jackson looked back at me and smirked.

I was furious. "Judge, that question has not been asked, and it's not been answered. I challenge the court to read the record. As a matter of fact, I *want* it read. I'm not going to ask another question until the court goes back through the record and finds out that that question has neither been asked nor answered."

Jackson sighed and looked at the jury. "Ladies and gentlemen, we're going to take a little recess. You may go out in the hall. I'll call you back when we're ready to continue." He glared at me and said for the jury to hear, "Mr. Richardson, I want to see *you* in my chambers."

Then he smiled and lowered his voice. "Mr. Caldwell, you may join us, if you'd like."

In chambers, Jackson exploded. "Richardson, I don't appreciate your conduct one whit. I won't put up with it. If you ever do anything like that again in my courtroom another eruption — I'll summon the sheriff and have you locked up so fast you won't know which direction is North." He glared at me.

"You understand me?" he demanded.

"Yes, your honor."

"Do you understand me?" he emphasized.

"Yes, sir."

"All right, then let's go back to the courtroom and get this case over with."

The first quality of courage
is the willingness to launch with no guarantees.

The second quality of courage
is the ability to endure
when there is no success in sight.
— Brian Tracy

I felt compelled to make my record, regardless of what might happen to me personally. "Just a minute, judge. I have listened carefully to what you have said. I would appreciate you extending the same courtesy to me."

I stepped toward him nodding my head.

"I think that I know why you're upset with me. It's because you ordered me to reduce this case to a misdemeanor, and I wouldn't do it. I assume that you feel that I have somehow not shown the respect for the court that I should. But that was not my intention. It is just that you don't have the authority to tell the District attorney's office how to handle our cases. It's not right for you to tell us to prosecute or not. That's our discretion. The people of this county have elected Mr. Fite to make that decision. But, if you did have that authority, I would certainly comply with what you asked. But as long as I'm in this position as an assistant District Attorney and, I have an obligation to the state of Oklahoma to stand up for the rights of the people. And I must do so.

Judge Jackson glared at me as I continued. "And I want to say this: You have threatened me. You've told me that if I repeat what I did in your courtroom, you're going to have me locked up. It's obvious you're trying to intimidate me. My suggestion to you, sir, is if you intend to continue to do what you've been doing during the trial, and that is to give me bad rulings- and sir, you know they're bad rulings- I don't think I have the ability to contain myself. I suggest that you cite me for contempt of court, call a mistrial, summon the sheriff, and have me locked up. My decision is firm. Whenever I'm in the courtroom, I'm going to see to it that the state gets a fair trial as best as I can, and if you intend to see to it that we don't, I'm headed to jail anyway."

I stopped, took a breath and met his stare. "If I should go to jail, I only want one phone call, and it won't be to my lawyer. It will be to the newspaper."

Judge Jackson was furious but from the look in his eyes I knew I had captured his attention. What I was doing was right, and he knew it. He nodded curtly and indicated with a scooping motion of his hands that we should go back to the courtroom.

Once we resumed the trial, the judge completely reversed his trend of bad rulings towards the state. From that moment, he more consistently overruled Caldwell's objections and sustained mine. I think he was convinced that I was willing to go to jail to see that the state get a fair trial, which, of course, I was.

Throughout the proceedings, Donald Wright's wife sat holding their baby on the front row of the courtroom. They complemented the devoted family-man appearance Wright had maintained everyday in court. In his closing argument, Sam Caldwell took advantage of this contrived domestic scene and told the jury that "All Mr. Richardson wants to do is take a fine man out of his home, away from his loving wife and new baby."

"Ladies and gentlemen of the jury," I countered, "I think Mr. Caldwell has his information mixed up. It's not about my taking anybody out of his home. Donald Wright made that decision when he broke into Dr. Fite's house. He made that decision. He decided he was willing to be taken out of his home away from his wife and child. He took the risk by stealing from innocent people. Those are the facts for your consideration."

As I mentioned earlier, one of our key witnesses had been Wright's nephew, who'd been involved in many of his uncle's capers. Caldwell had done his best to discredit the young man. However, I was optimistic that if the jury accepted the nephew's story, they would conclude that Donald Wright had committed the burglary.

After the jury retired to deliberate, I was standing in the hallway outside the district attorney's office, one floor down from the courtroom. Out of the corner of my eye, I noticed Wright had come down to the D.A.'s floor. He stopped some twenty feet away and looked at me. I sensed that he wanted to talk. Finally, he motioned for me to come near.

"Well, Mr. Richardson," he said when I reached his side, "I want to tell you two things. First, you don't have any business being a prosecutor. With your style of communication and fervor, you ought to be a Baptist preacher. The way you make a closing argument, all worked up and sure of yourself, you ought to be thumping a Bible and spreading the Gospel." I smiled hearing his sincerity. "Second," he went on, "I want to congratulate you for doing what nobody else has ever been able to do. You're going to get me convicted."

I raised my eyebrows at that statement. "Donald, it's a little early to say that. You never know what a jury will do."

Wright shook his head slowly. "No, I've been in enough trials to know when I've been had." He tapped his index finger against my chest. "But in the unlikely event there's a hung jury, Gary, I would like for you to make a commitment to me."

"What's that?"

"That you won't prosecute me next time. Let one of the other assistants do it."

I replied earnestly, "I can give you a commitment, but I'm afraid it's not the one you're asking for. I'll commit to you that as long as I'm a prosecutor in this county, and as long you're breaking the law in this county, I will do everything I can to put you behind bars. You need to know that. It's not personal with me. But it's my job, and I will do it to the best of my ability."

Wright met me eye to eye. There seemed to be not only a look of anxiety but a look of relief as well. I wondered how long he had lived his life on the edge knowing that at some moment he would surely get kicked off.

"Donald," I continued, "if you do lose and go to the penitentiary, you could use that time to make something positive out of your life. You could study great books, one of them being the Bible and become more of what you were meant to be. This could be a real chance for you to get your life right with God and society. When you get out, you could be a real witness to young people about getting straight."

"The jury's back," a voice called out.

Wright and I went back to the courtroom together and stood waiting for the verdict. The foreman handed a folded slip of paper to Judge Jackson. He opened it and considered it for a few seconds.

"Guilty," he read.

The punishment was set at five years in the state penitentiary at McAlester. Before Wright was led away, I leaned across the table toward him. "Donald, you're a fortunate man. You could have gotten fifteen. Use these five years to create a new life for you, your wife, and your child."

I'm convinced that, over the years, pleas and pay offs had kept Donald Wright out of jail. I don't know if he ever killed anyone, but chances are his "associates" certainly could have.

District Attorney Julian Fite embraced me after the verdict. He was thrilled.

"Fantastic job, Gary," he exclaimed. Then he shook my hand and thanked me again. His relief at the outcome radiated from the broad smile on his face.

I knew that he had been worried about losing the case, especially because it involved his uncle. Fite was a good man to work for. He gave me the responsibility to conduct our part of the trial, he let me do my job without interference, and we won. As a young prosecutor, I'd made my boss happy, and I felt justice was served in the process. I was on top of the world.

After his release from prison, years later, Wright never committed another crime in Muskogee County that we knew. I now believe that his burglary of Dr. Fite's home was his last offense in our jurisdiction. Most of his activity had been out of state. After he served his time in Oklahoma, I understand he was indicted and convicted of rape elsewhere and was sentenced to prison for life. He may even be dead today.

I never had any further problems with Judge Billy Jack Jackson after the Donald Wright trial. As a matter of fact, in addition to friendly exchanges in the courtroom, he occasionally called me to his chambers to discuss issues. I know he saw my sincerity and came to respect it.

I think Billy Jack was a good judge. There was never any hint of personal impropriety. I wasn't discouraged by his attitude towards me during the Wright case because he really might have believed that reducing the criminal charge was correct and that pursuing a felony conviction was a waste of time. However, I have to say that I felt that Judge Jackson, like many judges, suffered from an erroneous attitude- that he was entitled to run everything in the courtroom. I have spent my career fighting for what I believe to be the best of what this country stands for. Maybe not always right, but always fighting for what I believe to be right.

It is one of the most beautiful compensations of life, that no man can sincerely try to help another without helping himself.
— Ralph Waldo Emerson

CHAPTER 3

DON'T BANK ON IT

Little People, A Larger Loan, Big Trouble

In early 1980, I received a telephone call that led to one of the worst cases I've ever had to deal with in my life. I nearly ended up in jail for standing up for my client's rights, and in retrospect, I'm awfully lucky I wasn't tossed in the hoosegow for my efforts.

While I was an assistant district attorney in Muskogee, I'd won 21 of 22 trials, losing only the first case I handled. When I struck out on my own, I'd done so in order to broaden my civil litigation practice. Even though I had built a successful career as a state prosecutor, I really hadn't enjoyed the daily grind of criminal practice. But what lay ahead made me question my decision to change my career direction.

That phone call came from Gene Steele, an unassuming man in his early sixties who lived with his wife, Sallie, in Abbott, Texas, a small town about fifteen miles north of Waco. At the time, my dad was pastor of a church in west Texas, and he had months earlier recommended me to the Steele's son, Rocky, who had been in a car wreck. I successfully handled the son's case, so his father called me for help when a Waco bank ruined their family business.

Gene and Sallie Steele were typical, hardworking country folks. They were slow-talking, not well educated, and at the lower end of middle-class, but street smart. Mr. Steele had graying chestnut hair that matched his khaki clothes. He didn't wear a cowboy hat or boots, but his accent was pure Texas drawl, and he never seemed to be in a hurry. Mrs. Steele was a slight, homely looking woman who was the perfect, American Gothic match for her husband. The Steele's had a mom-and-pop business, called Tac Air, which they operated out of a small building in their backyard. They sold staple guns, staples, and other supplies to furniture manufacturers and upholsterers.

For four years, the Steele's had maintained three loans at Citizens National Bank in Waco, totaling about $15,000, with the Tac Air accounts receivable as collateral. The loan agreements provided that if the bank ever became *"insecure"* about the Steele's ability to repay the money the bank could call the accounts receivable. One day, out of the blue, Citizens National, the major bank in town, strongly requested that the Steele's consolidate their three loans into one, and, even more curiously, encouraged them to increase the amount of the new loan to $25,000.

What the bank didn't tell the couple was that Texas had just passed a law that gave banks Draconian rights over loans of $25,000 or more. Citizens National took immediate advantage of the new law and persuaded the unsuspecting Steele's into increasing their loan to that amount. Gene and Sallie didn't need the extra money at the time, but they went along. Shortly thereafter, the paperwork had been signed, the bank accelerated the due date — even though Mr. And Mrs. Steele had made timely payments and their loans had never been in default.

Mr. and Mrs. Steele were aghast. They frantically attempted to get the bank to restore the original terms. They had been good customers for years, and they felt betrayed, but Citizens National was unyielding. It telephoned all of Tac Air's accounts and instructed them to pay the bank instead of the Steeles. What this did, of course, was to create doubt and confusion among Tac Air's customers and, worse, to dry up the Steele's cash flow, preventing them from paying their daily operating expenses and suppliers. From the appropriate documents on file at the bank, Citizens National knew the Tac Air's financial condition in detail and fully realized that calling the note would force them out of business. In effect, Citizens National intentionally, in calling the note, created an intolerable situation that prevented the Steeles from meeting their loan commitment. In desperation, they decided to sue the bank. They had never before taken such action. As a matter of fact, they had never been in court for anything.

The wheels of justice sometimes grind slowly. In the Steele's case they barely seemed to move at all. For two years, Gene Steele waited for his day in court. As time passed, he began to worry that there wouldn't ever be a trial. The problem, which he hadn't anticipated, was that he couldn't keep an attorney. One by one, five lawyers, all from the Waco area, accepted the case, worked on it for a while, took his money, then gave it back, telling him that he didn't have a good lawsuit. At first, Mr. Steele was inclined to believe the reasons the lawyers gave for withdrawing from his case, saying that they had concluded the Bank's conduct didn't constitute a legal wrong, in their opinion. Up to that point, they had made their hourly wages from the Steeles of $200 to $300 per hour. Then, after considerable reflection, he became convinced that the real reason the Waco attorneys had bailed out had more to do with local politics than with the legitimacy of his case.

I was the sixth lawyer Gene Steele hired, and I agreed almost immediately with his conclusion. It was apparent that the Waco lawyers started feeling the pressure and controversy of going against the "power structure" and the most influential financial institution in town, and, once the heat was on, they all withdrew. In addition, Walter Lacy, the bank president, was a Waco "institution" himself and had a reputation for doing people wrong. As in many communities, a handful of people ran Waco. Each morning, the powers-that-be met in the coffee shop next to the bank, drank coffee and smoked cigars, and decided the city's destiny, so the rumor went.

I can't blame those local attorneys for not wanting to stir up a hornet's nest in their own backyard. After all, most small-town lawyers can make good money without taking on controversial cases, so it's just easier to walk away from a lawsuit like Mr. Steele's. But it can also mean the denial of justice.

Steele v. Citizens National Bank was my first trial away from home, and any notions I might have had that Black Robe Fever was limited to Muskogee County were quickly dispelled. I was about to learn that judges who decide to violate the Code of Judicial Conduct are not at all choosy about where they live or where they practice their malevolence. Small town or big city, major lawsuit or not, it seems to make no difference.

I took the case because I felt that Mr. and Mrs. Steele had been abused. Since I was a child, I had been described as one that would always get involved if I thought someone was being abused. I knew it would be a tough battle, but I had never backed away from a formidable fight since at age 15 my dad learned that I was running from a bully and said to me "no son of mine will ever be a coward." It was years later before I came to realize how that one statement, from a man that I so loved and admired, would so greatly impact my life. Nor, did I understand that leading the opposition in the Steele case would come more from the man in the black robe than from the defense lawyers. After all, this was a bank, a bank that belonged to one of Waco's most powerful men. And, I was at that time in my career very naïve about the power and control that this would have over our judge. What a learning experience I was in for, not about the law, but about the significance of the power outside the courtroom that comes into the courtroom thru political involvement.

"Five lawyers have already told you that you don't have a good case," I forewarned Mr. Steele, "so it could be that you don't have a good case." The average person would have given up after one lawyer dropped his case, much less five, but not Gene Steele. I had the feeling he would have retained five more attorneys if I hadn't come on board. He wasn't overly aggressive, but he wouldn't quit when he'd set his mind. He'd been reading law books at the courthouse, and he was ready for battle. At the end of our first meeting, and in spite of his resolve, I cautioned him that he shouldn't expect any miracles. I liked the case, but these were special circumstances. Since the lawsuit would be tried so far from home and I was a sole practitioner, I couldn't afford to run to Waco every time something came up. Many times a lawyer has to be at the courthouse for only thirty minutes or so for a short, not-so-important matter on a case. So I decided to get assistance from local counsel. It couldn't be just anybody, though. I needed someone who was unafraid of that local, established power base.

I found just what I was looking for in Vic Feazell (fuh-ZEL) a new Waco lawyer who was representing some of Steele's relatives. It was a needle-in-the-haystack discovery to find the kind of lawyer I needed to help me tackle the local power structure, especially in a city as small as Waco where practically everybody knew everybody else and five lawyers had backed out. For his part, Feazell took a heck of a risk to his brand-new practice by assisting me in representing Mr. and Mrs. Steele against Citizens National Bank. But he had only been out of Baylor Law School for about six months, and he was eager to serve justice. Feazell had already displayed his individuality and willingness to take on the establishment while a student at Baylor by running against an entrenched Waco city councilman. He didn't win, but he was beginning to make his mark on this community as a man who wasn't afraid to go against its ensconced regime. Vic later ran against the establishment District Attorney and won, becoming the County District Attorney and being the first outsider in recent years to topple the establishment. It reminded me of "how do you eat an elephant"? One bite at a time.

As I started working on the case, something happened which I have since found to be standard fare in all of my out-of-town trials: It didn't take long before the local attorneys and courthouse personnel began to volunteer information about other attorneys and judges in town. I was told, for example, that the lawyers for the bank, Dan Mayfield and Vance Dunnam, both of Waco, were good friends of 170th State District Judge Raymond Mormino, who would preside over the Steele matter. Now, the friendship of local lawyers with a local judge is not uncommon, especially in a small town, but it certainly doesn't make an out-of town lawyer's job any easier.

Judge Mormino was in his sixties. He was of medium height, about five feet ten inches tall, and he had dark wavy hair, touched with gray, which he combed straight back. Most people in Waco thought he was a war hero having been wounded while in combat, but, in reality, he had been in a stateside military plane crash during World War II. He'd been burned and was badly disfigured, with obvious scars on his face and hands. His ears were hardly more than nubs of flesh. The local talk was that his war-hero image kept getting him reelected, even though those close to Mormino knew the truth about his injuries. The judge himself did nothing to refute the myth. Several courtroom watchers opined that his unorthodox actions were a result of the pain he had experienced.

It was common knowledge in the law community that Mormino had few cases on his docket, and there was a reason why. Few lawyers wanted to appear before him and at that time, in that county, lawyers were free to pick and choose the judge they wanted. The judge could often be found roasting pecans on a little hot plate in his library where many of the retired lawyers in Waco would come to pass the day by sharing war stories and eating pecans with him.

Mormino's behavior was unconventional in more ways than one. Most judges use a gavel to call a court session to order and to get attention in the courtroom, but Mormino used a big carpenter's claw hammer to get the participants' attention. Evidence of his frequent poundings pitted his desktop.

Most lawyers were intimidated by the judge's volatile behavior and erratic demands. Accordingly, given a choice, they wouldn't willingly try a case before him. Waco, the county seat of McLennan County, was a large enough jurisdiction that they had a choice. Unlike any other place I knew of, when a lawsuit was filed in McLennan County, the filing attorney got to pick the judge for the trial

Because Mormino was cantankerous and unpredictable, few ever requested his courtroom, so he had plenty of time to roast pecans. In any event, when he did work, he was stuck with all the welfare and child-support cases that the other judges didn't want to be bothered with. Steele v. Citizens National Bank was assigned to him because the attorney who originally filed the lawsuit mailed it in and didn't indicate a preference. The court clerk must have thought, "Ahh, here's one we can give Judge Mormino to help balance the workload."

The court date was set shortly after I agreed to represent Gene Steele. I loaded my car with clothes and drove down to Waco, ready for trial. However, the bank's attorneys asked for a continuance, and, over my objection, Judge Mormino granted it. At first, I was annoyed, and then I realized the delay could be an asset. There had been very little work done on the case by Mr. Steele's previous lawyers, and the continuance would provide Feazell and me with more time to prepare. Also, when I took the case, the Steeles didn't have an expert witness to describe the damages they had suffered. I explained to them that we might get a much better verdict if we had an economist to testify on our behalf. Fortunately, we were able to hire one in time for the trial, who proved to be worthy of his hire.

The legal process is wonderful but complicated. To the uninitiated, it sometimes seems like a beast designed from one of those children's toys where you can put the head of a tiger onto the torso of a pig with the legs of a giraffe. There are many steps on the road to the final destination, which is of course, the trial.

In a civil matter, once the decision is made to sue and a lawyer has been hired, or vice versa, the next action is the filing of a petition in the forum that has jurisdiction over the dispute-the appropriate county, state, or federal court. This filing does not have to be done by the lawyer. Anybody can file a petition at the court clerk's office on behalf of the lawyer. There is a filing fee, which varies from court to court.

Then, the party being sued is served notice of the lawsuit. The defendant has twenty to thirty days, depending on the jurisdiction, to respond. Normally, once an answer by the party being sued has been filed, either by themselves or their lawyer is made, the discovery process begins. However, the defendant might first move to dismiss the case, saying, for example, that there is no basis for it. If such a motion fails, the discovery process begins. There will be depositions, interrogatories, and requests for admissions and documents. Once this step is completed, the case is ready for the courtroom trial, typically with a jury. Sometimes, as happened in the Steele case, when all parties appear on the designated trial date, the defense requests a continuance, which frequently is granted, postponing the day when all parties finally step into the courtroom to begin the trial. Most plaintiffs have a difficult time understanding these delays, and they aren't the only ones. Granting a continuance generally plays havoc with the plans of their lawyers as well.

Waco, a city of about 100,000 people, is located in the beautiful hill country of central Texas, halfway between Dallas and Austin. It lies in a gentle valley covered with oak and cedar trees and is home to Baylor University, the Southern Baptists' largest university. During the summer, Waco can be unmercifully hot and humid, but its winters tend not to be severely cold. The one major exception to that trend was the winter of 1980 when our lawsuit finally went to trial. The weather was bitterly frigid, and the wind cut through even the bulkiest protection. The biggest seller around town everyday was steaming hot coffee. Shivering customers sat at restaurant counters and held their cups with both hands and numbly mouthed occasional comments about Mother Nature's unusual wrath.

Vic Feazell's office was about a block away from the courthouse, but it seemed like a country mile as we carried briefcases and boxes of files through the icy blast from the north.

The cold weather was a harbinger of the treatment we were about to receive in the courtroom of Judge Raymond Mormino. Right before the trial, the lawyers for both sides had a conference with the judge. Dunnam and Mayfield, the bank's attorneys, brought up the fact that Gene Steele had retained five other lawyers, all locals, before hiring me, an "outsider." I immediately asked the judge to rule that such information had nothing to do with the lawsuit and therefore wasn't admissible. Mormino agreed and instructed the two lawyers that they could not bring this up during trial. So far, so good, I thought. With that potential and inappropriate bombshell out of the way, the trial began.

Part of our strategy was to show that Citizens National bank had a hidden agenda when they called the Steele's note. We felt circumstances showed that the bank had no reason to be insecure and was camouflaging whatever the real reason was by using the "insecure" excuse to foreclose on the Steeles. Then our expert witness, the economist, explained to the jury the type of damage our clients had suffered because of the bank's conduct. At one point, the bank's attorneys attempted to characterize our clients as lawbreakers because when authorities had gone to the Steele home to seize assets, their son Rocky, six feet tall, stood in the door and wouldn't let them in. But this ploy boomeranged when Rocky, slowly and with tears in his eyes, defended his actions by saying he was only trying to protect what little his father had left to make a living for his mother and younger sister.

By the second day of the trial, it was obvious to everyone in the courtroom that we were making direct hits against the defense. I could see it in the eyes of the jurors and spectators. When Judge Mormino realized that our chances of winning were clearly better than anyone expected, black robe fever kicked in. He stepped in abruptly to attempt to reverse the direction the case was going-at least to halt the momentum. From this point forward he did everything he could to make life miserable for us. As Feazell later put it, "Judge Mormino was on our rears constantly."

The defense attorneys representing the bank, Dunnam and Mayfield, could make any kind of objection they wanted, no matter how far-fetched it might be, and Mormino would regularly rule in their favor. At one point, Mayfield catapulted out of his chair and pointed at Vic.

"Mr. Feazell is smirking."

I had never heard *that* objection before.

Mayfield continued. "When he thinks things are going well for their side, he sits over there and grins. He's trying to give messages to the jury with his facial expressions."

"Sustained," Mormino exclaimed.

Feazell defended himself by replying, "Your Honor, I can't help it. That's just the way I look."

The judge boomed, "I said, 'Sustained.'"

A few minutes later, during another exchange we had with the defense, Judge Mormino chastised Vic again, warning him to watch his facial expressions "or else."

But Mormino's coup de grace hit us when he reversed the ruling he had made before the trial started, when he had told the defense attorneys that they would not be allowed to bring up the fact that the Steele's had hired Vic and me as their fifth set of lawyers. The previous four firms, all from Waco, withdrew from their case, something that would obviously be damning to the case, and obviously not relevant or admissible, just as Judge Mormino knew when he made this ruling. Yet, he later changed this ruling when it became obvious that we were winning.

Gene Steele was on the stand for cross examination when one of the bank's attorneys asked something like, "Mr. Steele, Mr. Richardson is not the lawyer who originally filed this lawsuit for you, is he?"

"No," answered my client.

"Well, who was the lawyer?"

I stood up and objected.

Mormino overruled me and told Mr. Steele to answer the question. For a second, I thought we might be all right if that were as far as the questioning went.

"How come he's no longer your lawyer, Mr. Steele? Did he withdraw, or did you fire him?"

"Objection!" I yelled.

Mormino overruled me again, gave me a stem look, and insisted on an answer.

"He, uh, withdrew."

"And what did he say to you when he withdrew from your case, Mr. Steele?"

There are two problems with this question. First, it isn't relevant, and second, it violates the attorney-client privilege.

"Objection!" I protested. "It isn't relevant. It isn't admissible. And, your Honor, I'd like to point out that you have previously sustained a motion instruction Mr. Dunnam and Mr. Mayfield that they cannot ask about Mr. Steele's other lawyers."

"Well, I'm reversing it, Mr. Richardson," Mormino coldly informed me.

Gene Steele was instructed to answer the question. In addition, the judge opened the door to the defense's inquiries about every other lawyer my client had ever had in this case.

Before Mr. Steele could say anything, I began screaming objections. Mormino angrily motioned me to the bench and told me, in essence, threatened me that if I ever again raised my voice in objection to his rulings, he would jail me at the end of the trial.

"Do you understand me?" he growled. He shook his claw hammer for emphasis.

I looked him in the eyes. "Judge Mormino, I'm not sure I did understand you. Would you mind repeating that?"

You know exactly what I said," he snarled as he positioned the hammer an inch from my nose.

"Yes, I do," I declared, "and I also know why. The reason is obvious: You're trying to control the verdict. You know that I represent some little folks who don't have the money to appeal this case of they lose, and you're trying every way you can to help the defense win this case. I'm going to tell you now that if you let Mr. Mayfield and Mr. Dunnam ask Mr. Steele about another lawyer, I'm going to raise the roof in this courtroom again. And when this case is over, if you feel that I should be jailed - and, yes, you have the authority to do it - then I will accept that. But as long as I'm in your courtroom representing these people, I'm going to do everything I can to see to it that they get justice.

I sat down, and, incredibly, Mormino let Dunnam ask Mr. Steele about another lawyer.

"Objection!" I roared. "It's irrelevant and immaterial."

The judge pounded his claw hammer as if he were attempting to demolish the top of his trial bench.

"Get up here!" he demanded.

At the bench, he chewed me out again. I shook my head. "Judge, the only way you're going to stop me from objecting is either to quit letting them ask about my client's previous lawyers or remove me from the courtroom."

He didn't do either so I continued my outbursts.

When we walked out of the courtroom that day, Feazell had a grim look on his face. "Well, that's it," he said, "We're through."

"No, we're not," I told him. "We're going to figure out a way to make them regret what they did. Did you see the jurors' reaction?" I asked.

I knew that the jury picked up on Mormino's prejudice when he arbitrarily reversed his ruling, thus sending a message that he was siding with the defense. It made it look as if the issue about local lawyers being unwilling to represent the Steeles was so important that even the district judge thought we didn't have a good case against the bank. Jurors usually believe whatever action a judge takes is right and therefore warranted, yet they were put on alert when a dramatic shift occurred in the judge's behavior. Something was going on there, something not right; not fair.

Mormino's action genuinely saddened me. Judges take an oath to be totally impartial in a trial. Showing preference to one side or the other violates that oath. What Mormino did by allowing obviously inadmissible evidence to be introduced for the purpose of damaging my client made a mockery of the Code of Judicial Conduct.

Attorneys know that many judges determine very early in a case what they believe the outcome should be. Some do this even before the trial begins. They have read the case file, and they develop an attitude. Unfortunately, more than a few are not mature enough to keep that attitude from influencing what goes on in the courtroom. If I am before a judge who is hell-bent on attempting to direct a case, I will work at communicating to the jury that this judge is trying to prejudice the case. That is the tactic I had to employ on Gene Steele's behalf. Generally, people are for the underdog and I went to work helping the jury see what we were up against, with this judge, who was a great example of "Black Robe Fever" at work in the courtroom.

###

At the close of the evidence portion of a trial, the judge gives instructions to the jurors, which are directives to follow in determining a verdict. In state court, this is usually done before closing arguments. Both sides prepare what they think the jury should be told, and then the judge forms *his* message, *the court's* instructions to the jury. He does this before the lawyers give their closing arguments.

Feazell and I spent an entire day with Judge Mormino and opposing counsel, working on the jury instructions. I made sure that ours was carefully worded so that we could submit a legally perfect charge. Mormino rewarded our labors by attacking our document with his scissors, muttering as he cut out portions he didn't like: "Well, you don't need this." He'd snip. "Or this, either." He snipped again. Finally, he taped the surviving parts to a separate piece of paper. The result looked as if rats had chewed on it. Many of the points we wanted were gone, and those Dunnam and Mayfield wanted were prominently included. The revised instructions to the jury required us to prove things to win our case that we didn't legally have to prove. We were going to have to make our final argument with a nearly insurmountable burden of proof.

After I read Judge Mormino's cobbled-together instructions, I turned to opposing counsel Vance Dunnam who was seated next to me.

"We just got screwed."

Dunnam laughed. His exact words were, "No, you just got f----d!"

It infuriated me that it was so obvious that the opposition was even willing to admit his prejudice. Mormino wanted to make it as difficult as he could for us to get a successful verdict for our clients.

"I'll tell you one thing, Vance," I vowed. "I will bring you, and your house of cards down tomorrow, and I will bet you that we get at least a $500,000 verdict."

"You're crazy," Dunnam responded.

"I may be, but I'm crazy enough to make the bet."

Dunnam grinned. "In that case, I'll bet you the biggest steak in town."

"Hey, don't make it easy on yourself," I told him.

"You bet whatever you want, and I'll call it."

I knew that odds were definitely in Dunnam's favor in view of what the judge had done to us throughout the trial and especially in the "instructions". As far as the defense was concerned, we were only talking about a $25,000 matter. Moreover, the defense had contended throughout that the bank hadn't done anything wrong. However, I believed that the jury would take into account the sordid fact that Citizens National Bank had destroyed the Steeles' small enterprise and that the judge denied us a level playing field. I don't know why I believed it so strongly, but I felt that in spite of Judge Mormino and his black robe fever, we would win.

There wasn't much time to construct a comeback.

Closing arguments were the following day.

The next morning, a Friday, while I was showering, I suddenly remembered an incident that had occurred on the first morning I was in Waco, when I was ready to go to trial, when Judge Mormino granted the defense a continuance. I decided that by relating that incident I might just be able to communicate to the jury why the Steeles had lost five lawyers and had to go out of state to secure representation. I finished getting ready and headed for the courthouse. I knew my closing statement would be all or nothing.

The walk from my motel was cold and long. I hoped it wasn't a harbinger of things to come.

Finally, when it was time, I walked closer to the jury and started.

"Folks, one thing I want to say to you is how impressed I've been with the job that these two defense lawyers have done. As a matter of fact, I want the two of them to know they deserve the reputation they have in this community. You know, I was down here a few weeks ago, standing out in the courthouse hallway, and being an obvious stranger to the other lawyers in town, a local lawyer recognizing me as a stranger, walked up to me, and learning that I was from Oklahoma, inquired as to what brought me to Waco. I told him I was here to represent the Steele family from the small town of Abbot, just north of Waco, against the local Waco Bank.

He asked me, "Who's the lawyer on the other side?"

"Well, they have two," I told him. "One's a fellow named Vance Dunn."

"Vance Dunnam?" he asked and backed up a step.

"Yeah."

"Are you kidding?"

"No. Then there's another one named Mayberry."

"Mayfield?"

"Yeah, that's it."

He backed up another step to say, "You're kidding."

I frowned. "I don't understand what you are saying, and why would I be kidding?"

"Don't you know who those lawyers are?"

"No," I replied hesitantly, "I've never heard of either one of them. As a matter of fact, I've never even met them personally."

I paused a moment not knowing what else to say.

Then he said, "Mr. Richardson, those two lawyers will eat your lunch."

"And folks, I want to tell you something. They've done a pretty good job of it. They've taken a case that didn't have a defense, and I'll be honest with you, they almost put one together. But fortunately for my clients, Mr. And Mrs. Steele, those lawyers didn't get there, I know they didn't, and I know you know they didn't. You understand now why the Steeles had to go all the way to Oklahoma to get a lawyer who would come down here and come into this courtroom and go up against these two lawyers, up against this big bank across the street, and —" I turned around and looked at the judge for several seconds, without saying a word.

The jury got the message. They deliberated for two hours and forty minutes before unanimously finding in favor of Gene Steele. The award was set at $695,000 - $670,000 for actual damages and $25,000 in punitive damages. During the reading of the verdict, I was happy as could be, but I kept my composure. Vic Feazell's eyes and mouth were wide open. I leaned over and whispered to him, "Don't overreact, or they'll think we've never had a big verdict like this before," which was, in fact, the case. At the time, it was the largest verdict ever awarded in McLennan County.

After the court was adjourned, Dunnam and Mayfield bolted for the door in a huff. The members of the jury filed out and stood in the hall and waited to tell Vic and me how proud they were that we had been willing to represent the Steeles. There were hugs and congratulations all around, except of course, from Dunnam and Mayfield, who stood by themselves and acted as if they didn't notice the emotional reaction.

Feazell and I headed back to his office. As we turned a corner, I looked around and saw that no one was on the street. I leapt about three feet in the air, waved my fists, and shouted, "Whoopee!" The suddenness of my jubilation startled Vic so much that he almost jumped out of his shoes. I grinned and told him, "Nobody saw that."

I wish I could say that the case ended here and that the Steeles received what the jury awarded them. It didn't, and they didn't.

Whether or not the verdict would stand was to be determined by Judge Mormino ten days after a judgment-not-withstanding-the-verdict motion was filed in district court. A lot more happened before it was all over. There were more motions and hearings, and a witness for the plaintiff, Mr. Steele's nephew, was shot at on his way to the courthouse for one of the sessions, obviously in attempt to intimidate him so he wouldn't testify. In another hearing after the trial, a witness for the bank became so angry with me during cross-examination when I attacked his credibility that he literally rose from the witness chair to come after me. He was a known wife-beater, and I had stated that he couldn't be trusted to tell the truth. It was a highly inflammatory situation. That episode, combined with the shooting incident, alerted Mormino to the tension surrounding the case. So some sixty days after the jury delivered the verdict, when I had to return to Waco for another hearing, Judge Mormino ordered guards posted around the courtroom because of the tension and the threats.

It took another six months to close the case. For some reason, Mormino still had not approved the judgment. A case cannot even be appealed until the order is signed, and we were concerned that because of the judge's conduct during the trial and rulings that were obviously incorrect, the only way for him to save face and avoid having the Court of Appeals "grade his papers" properly was for him to reverse the jury's verdict and grant a new trial. Either that or reduce the verdict so low that the Steeles would be forced to accept practically nothing. So, reluctantly, we made the decision that after all the Steeles had been through, it was better to make certain they got something rather than nothing. We settled the Steele case for a little over a hundred thousand dollars, substantially less than the amount set by the jury. In a nutshell, we did so because we became convinced that Judge Mormino was likely to overturn the verdict and grant a new trial on the basis that he himself had given a flawed charge to the jury.

It would have been the height of irony for us to suffer that fate after prevailing over his prejudiced instructions.

I might add that Mormino's entire attitude toward me changed after the verdict. Apparently, I had gained his respect by showing respect for him even when I stood my ground. After the trial, there was no further mention of my going to jail. I was later hired for several other cases in Waco, and there were times when Mormino might hear me talking in his courtroom, and call from his chambers, "Is that my Oklahoma lawyer out there?" He became very friendly toward me. Unfortunately, that wasn't the case for Feazell, who continued to practice law in Waco for several years. "Judge Mormino hated my guts for the rest of the time I was in that courthouse," he told me, "and it was very obvious."

There also was a weird twist to my involvement in Steele v. Citizens National Bank. Taking that case probably saved my life. I say that because I was also representing the Steeles' nephew in a property dispute, and both cases were set for trial on the same day. I had to withdraw from one, so I chose to represent Gene Steele because he had hired me first. The lawyer who replaced me in the nephew's case narrowly escaped death, or at least serious injury, when one of the parties in that trial stabbed him in the back with a large butcher's knife. I could have been the victim if I hadn't been representing Gene Steele, and I might not have been as lucky as the other lawyer.

Throughout the years since the Steele case, I have tried many lawsuits away from home. I now actually prefer to do so. If I'm out of town, my total being can be concentrated on the matter at hand. But if I'm at home, I have the usual distractions of everyday life. Your family expects you to be "normal," which is impossible for me if a major trial looms before me. Also, I have a lot easier time challenging the forces out of town than I do at home. I'm more willing to take on a judge miles away. I don't like to go to local bar association meetings and run into a jurist with whom I've just had a strong confrontation. If I have to do that I will, but it's just a lot easier to make my enemies out of town then come back home where I can live a more peaceful life.

I've always wanted to help people in trouble. When I do so, most everything else seems to become secondary.

However, I have to admit that during <u>Steele v. Citizens National Bank</u>, my first out-of-town case, there were many times when I asked my self, "Is it worth it to drive ten hours to stand up for the rights of virtual strangers?" Then, I remember Gene and Sallie Steele, sitting in my office with tears in their eyes, pleading with me to represent them.

My answer today is the same as it was to them: "Absolutely."

CHAPTER 4

OFFICIAL VENDETTA

When the Good Guys Wear Black Hats

"When you piss off the Texas Rangers," a former state prosecutor once quipped, "they'll start a war."

In the fall of 1984, two years after Vic Feazell was elected district attorney of McLennan County, Texas, that's exactly what he did, and the notorious lawmen more than lived up to their part of the bargain.

Feazell, my co-counsel in the Steele case, didn't know it at the time, but his honestly expressed skepticism about the guilt of a drifter accused of multiple murders produced a vicious, seven-year attack on his personal and professional reputation. He was unjustly vilified, pursued, and indicted by government agents whose sworn duty was to uphold the law. In Vic's case, they not only did not uphold the law, but FBI agents, sheriff Boutwell, Chief Adams who headed the Texas Rangers and was formerly number three in the FBI in Washington, DC, and numerous other law enforcement officers prostituted the law as confirmed by the verdict in the Feazell criminal trial as well as interviews by the jurors following their verdict. Still, Vic's horror story was an agonizing and unrelieved odyssey of retaliation and persecution, which finally ended with his complete vindication, and, later, our winning on Vic's behalf the largest libel verdict in American history against the Belo Corporation, one of the largest media conglomerates in the United States of America.

Two hundred and fifty years ago, the French political philosopher Baron de Montesquieu wrote, "There is no crueler tyranny than that which is perpetuated under the shield of law and in the name of justice."

What happened to Vic Feazell was the most egregious example of official misconduct I have ever witnessed.

###

Victor Fred Feazell, as a line in that old song goes, "was the son of a preacher man." His father, an itinerant Baptist minister, carried the Gospel from town to town as their family moved across Louisiana and Texas. Fred Feazell genuinely wanted young Vic to follow in his footsteps, and, for a while, that path seemed to be assured. Feazell became active in his father's church efforts, and, when he was 13, he delivered his first sermon during a youth worship service. However, in high school, at Leander, Texas, he became more interested in girls, cars, and hunting than the ministry, but, in deference to his dad's wishes, he continued to serve an occasional stint as an assistant in the pulpit.

Vic graduated from high school shortly before his seventeenth birthday with his eyes fixed on a career in law enforcement. He enrolled in a cadet training program sponsored by the Austin Police Department, and, shortly afterwards, he began attending Mary Hardin-Baylor College in Belton, a small town between Austin and Waco. There, he performed odd jobs around the campus, doing landscaping and maintenance work in exchange for the opportunity to attend classes. After graduation, Vic didn't hesitate. He applied for and was granted admission to Baylor Law School in Waco. To pay the steep, three-year tuition, he worked in juvenile probation and, on occasion, took further advantage of the skills he had acquired from his father. He preached.

When Feazell obtained his law degree and passed the Texas bar exam in 1979, he thoughtfully considered the various localities where he might establish his practice. Everyone advised that the best opportunities were in Dallas and Houston, but Vic's period of introspection was short lived. It quickly foundered on the shoals of reality - he was too broke to relocate. Fortunately, his year of apprenticeship at his father's side had honed his gift of persuasion and his flair for the dramatic. So, in spite of his bleak financial situation, he was able to borrow $5,000 to set up his own office in Waco. True to his nature as one who prided himself in not being a "joiner," Vic started a solo law practice. Having other attorneys scurrying around, he concluded, would only be distracting and would prevent him from doing what he called, "my own thing."

Vic's wife, Bernadette, or "Berni," as most everyone called her, was a tall, auburn-haired woman who was fanatically devoted to her husband. She was aware that those who were acquainted with Vic called him flamboyant and theatrical. Clients loved him.

But Berni knew his private side, pensive and frequently dour in demeanor.

Over the years, Feazell had discovered and revered his heroes: "Kingfish" Huey P. Long, the Louisiana populist, Moses, David, Thomas Jefferson, Abraham Lincoln, and Lyndon Baines Johnson. All were celebrated activists, and he passionately wanted to emulate them. To do so, he realized, would necessitate a strategic change in the direction of his career.

Even though Feazell had been unsuccessful in an earlier run for city council while still attending law school at Baylor University, this time it was different. He now had that "fire in the belly." In spring of 1982, at age 31, he brashly announced that he would be a Democratic candidate for McLennan County District Attorney. For him, this was the big time. His decision pitted him against the incumbent, Felipe Reyna, who had been D.A. for six years. To the entrenched Reyna and virtually the entire party establishment, Feazell was considered "a political nuisance." However, he mounted a vigorous campaign directed toward middle-class and blue-collar voters against "society people" and "the power structure."

To the surprise of most everyone, other than himself and Berni, he won the May primary and the general election that fall. Vic Feazell took office in January of 1983.

Six months earlier, a tragic event took place, which symbolically marked the beginning of the personal hell Feazell was to endure for nearly a decade.

Late on the steamy evening of July 13, 1982, three teenagers — a boy and two girls — were savagely murdered in a remote lakeside park outside Waco. Their bound and bloodied bodies bore a total of forty-eight stab wounds, most of which, the coroner reported, were deep punctures followed by wide slashes, indicating a maniacal fury on the part of the killer. Many of the stabs, most probably the first ones inflicted on the victims, were not intended to kill but, rather, to torture. Someone had wanted the teenagers to die after suffering inconceivable agony. The throat of one of the girls was slashed so completely that she had nearly been decapitated. In addition, one of her nipples had been bitten off.

Both girls had been sexually violated. This unspeakable deed was the worst multiple homicide ever in central Texas.

After the Waco Police Department gave up its months-long pursuit of leads in the Lake Waco case, the McLennan County Sheriff's Department continued and finally narrowed its focus on three men: David Spence, Gilbert Melendez, and Gilbert's brother, Tony. David Spence was termed a master manipulator and a con artist even by those who knew him casually. His principal liability was his violent personality, which could be provoked to rage, even to kill without remorse, upon a moment's stimulation.

Vic Feazell prosecuted the three accused men. All were convicted, and Spence was condemned to die at the state penitentiary at Huntsville. This apparent ending to a ghastly incident, however, was only a prologue to what lay ahead for Feazell. During and after Spence's trial, Russ Hunt, the ex-con's court-appointed lawyer, verbally attacked the D.A. with ferocity, which bordered on the fanatical. There were times when observers wondered if Hunt would attack Feazell physically. Hunt's actions might not have directly precipitated what was about to happen, but they were indeed a harbinger of things to come.

At about the time Feazell was concluding the Lake Waco murder trials, the Texas Rangers picked up an itinerant named Henry Lee Lucas who immediately began to confessing to murders all across the United States and Canada. Over time, he glibly admitted to as many as 600 killings. What got Feazell's attention was Lucas' assertion that he had slain two individuals in Waco. Vic had nearly completed the investigation of these other murders, and this new development, which, in his opinion was a wholly unsubstantiated allegation, threatened months of methodical work, as well as jeopardized the potential conviction of the person that District Attorney Feazell and his office had prepared to arrest for the murder, and who they believed the evidence showed to be guilty.

From his own efforts and tips from sources, including reporters, Feazell was certain that Lucas had nothing whatsoever to do with the homicides. The more he looked into some of the drifter's other confessions, he became convinced that most, if not all of them were probably concocted as well. His public expressions of doubt as to why the law enforcement community had been so quick to accept the validity of the confessions earned him the enmity of the men with the badges. What he did next almost sealed his fate.

Feazell contacted Texas Attorney General Jim Maddox and requested that a grand jury be called to investigate every one of the Lucas confessions. He didn't know it at the time, but the word had already spread throughout the ranks of the Texas Rangers that a "piss ant D.A." was in the process of attempting not only to undo Lucas' Waco confessions but also to destroy the credibility of their prized "catch," an unthinkable possibility which would jeopardize countless convictions. The potential fallout could be disastrous. Lawmen and prosecutors throughout North America had accepted Lucas' confession at face value, based entirely on the reputation of the bigger-than- life Texas Rangers, who had proudly led the task force, totally supported by Adams, the head of the Texas Rangers.

Feazell had stepped on some big toes, and their furious owners were going to make him pay for it. No one, not even another lawman, messed with this legendary organization and got away with it. The bureaucratic machinery began to grind. Feazell's attempt to expose Lucas as a fraud had to be stopped, one way or another.

Henry Lee Lucas had been picked up and jailed on a minor charge in 1983. Once in court, and after being "induced" to confessing to the supposed killing of Becky Powell, his former girlfriend, Lucas began talking freely about his remarkable "created" criminal career. It was a veritable litany of random murders, which he bragged he had committed in twenty-six states and Canada from 1976 to the present. Incredulous lawmen listened and encouraged their loquacious captive to unburden himself. This he did, naming dates and places (provided to him by law enforcement) where, in most instances, murders had indeed taken place. It was an embarrassment of riches, for it meant that hundreds of unsolved crimes could be closed out.

There were hundreds of inconsistencies, but they were no impediment to the overwhelming desire by law enforcement personnel to write "closed" on case files that had festered and angered residents of the various areas where the killings had occurred. Even the fact that Lucas owned up to several murders that had never happened wasn't sufficient to raise a warning flag. This train was on a roll, and everyone expected to come out a winner.

The Texas Rangers tightened their control over the Lucas matter and set up a task force in Georgetown, a little town north of Austin on Interstate 35. The word went out, and lawmen came from far and wide to interview and collect guilty pleas from this odd little man who seemed to be their salvation. This "salvation" came after Lucas was first provided with their investigation file that would have been sent to local Sheriff Boutwell's office where Lucas was housed. There the files would be given to Lucas to study before the officer doing the investigation would go to Georgetown and interview Lucas. Even though he had an IQ of 84 ranking him as "borderline retarded," no one seemed to wonder, or care, how he could relate the specifics of so many murders in such detail — often years after the crimes had been committed. Even the fact that some of his confessions were to offenses which took place at the same time, but hundreds of miles apart, caused no concern. Neither did the fact that there was never any physical evidence that Lucas had been nearby, nor that no one had witnessed his being at even one of the killings.

Regardless, in the flattering spotlight of international attention, the Rangers kept transporting Lucas to many of the sites where he'd said he'd killed people. He pointed here and there, and it all looked so believable to those who had no idea what was happening. It was a well-orchestrated charade, which was widely publicized. The public relations effect was glorious, and praise and commendations, even formal certificates, poured into the task force's headquarters.

It was all too much for Feazell. He arranged to meet with Lucas and was quickly able to gain his confidence. From the drifter's own mouth and other sources, Feazell obtained what he was looking for: incontrovertible evidence that numerous "confessions" by Lucas were fraudulent and he'd said so publicly. The infuriated Rangers retaliated and attacked his motivations. They cynically used Feazell's own term "fraudulent" to characterize his straightforward objections to their antics. They were so caught up in the glory; they had no mind to hear otherwise.

###

In January, 1985, when Vic Feazell drove the hundred miles to Austin to meet with Attorney General Maddox about the Lucas matter and the need for a grand jury to get to the bottom of it, the Department of Public Safety had already launched its own investigation of Feazell. Colonel Jim Adams, director of the DPS and commander of the Rangers, had called ahead to alert Maddox that Feazell was "a crazy" who could cause a lot of trouble.

Vic had recently learned that the Waco police department was investigating him. He had no clue as to the reason. Rumor had it that David Smith, Waco's city manager, had been a high school buddy of DPS's Adams, and he had apparently called for the local inquiry.

"Dig into everything since he's been in office," Smith reportedly ordered the police chief. "Make him look bad. I don't care how you do it. I don't like the way he's treating the Rangers."

Few in the Waco police department hierarchy had any respect for the district attorney who had frequently criticized their chief for abuses and the department's Drug Enforcement Unit for its tendencies toward violence. Even worse, in their eyes, Feazell, always insisted on legally appropriate procedures during drug raids. Present him with a defective warrant, and Vic would promptly dismiss the charge. Violators of his policies got short shrift.

The police took direct aim at Feazell's handling of driving-while-intoxicated cases. Despite the fact that the D.A. had one of the highest DWI conviction rates in the state, his occasional habit of "cutting some slack" even though a common practice in most all District Attorney Offices, was widely unpopular with the local cops.

"They'd bring in a first-time offender," Feazell reflected, "and, if I thought it probably wouldn't happen again, I'd suggest the guy waive his right to a speedy trial, tell him to keep his nose dry for a year, then I'd dismiss the charge," Feazell smiled. "The police wanted to jail just about everybody, but it wasn't always in the best interest of the accused ... or the community."

Unfortunately for Feazell, his policy turned out not to be in his own best interest either, when they were hunting something to try to nail him. Enraged members of the Waco Police Department and others who wanted Vic stopped contacted television station

WFAA in Dallas and alleged that Feazell's real motive was money, specifically, bribery. The police urged that the big-city electronic media come down and examine their records that would prove that the district attorney had accepted money in return for dismissing DWI charges. Other Waco "informants" who wanted Feazell strung up came forth and seconded the opinion. WFAA immediately dispatched a reporter, Charles Duncan, to investigate.

Duncan was one of the TV station's best, and he instantly recognized the career-making potential of exposing what came to appear to be a crooked D.A. Since he'd have the support not only of local lawmen, but the Texas Rangers as well, it would be a piece of cake with a lot of frosting. He arrived in Waco and eagerly sought out his sources. Over the next few weeks, Duncan made close friends in the department, which wasn't surprising given the fact that the police considered him a useful tool in their inquisition. The reporter rode around in patrol cars and sifted through official files. Behind Feazell's back, everything was made available to him. Nothing was off limits, even sealed records, which were, by court order, never to see the light of day much less be examined by a member of the media. However, the more Duncan probed, the more he saw there were two sides to most if not all of the cases. Some weren't cases at all.

One involved a 19-year old man who'd supplied liquor to his wife, a minor. This was perfectly legal, since by being married, the girl was considered an adult. Thus, no law had been broken. When the young man tried to explain this to the arresting officers, they'd punch him in the nose and broken his glasses for his unsolicited advice.

Then, there were dozens of people hauled in who hadn't consumed any alcohol or illegal drugs at all, but they "just looked like the type." It seemed like the police hierarchy wanted to make the district attorney look bad by forcing him to empty the jail and turn "criminals" loose. In addition, Duncan learned that Feazell had even been criticized for not prosecuting individuals who were never charged with anything in the first place. Finally, the WFAA reporter was given documents on a case, which had been expunged by court order. By itself, delivery of such material by the police to an outsider was a violation of the law.

As it turned out, the "investigation" by the Waco Police Department was mostly a ruse to scare Feazell from his pursuits. The chief and others had hoped to put out the fire while it was still contained. But, as Vic learned over the next three months, his hometown police were quite capable of playing hardball when Feazell refused to give up his search for the truth.

###

Feazell summoned a grand jury in McLennan County for April, 1985. Within days of the announcement, he learned just how serious the opposition was in blocking any meaningful revelations.

Threats were made against his life by anonymous callers, unmarked cars occupied by stem-looking men cruised past his home and throughout the neighborhoods of his friends around the clock, his garbage was stolen and presumably searched for incriminating evidence, and, after Vic's wife Berni noticed men climbing down a telephone pole in a nearby alley, the telephone company confirmed that someone had tampered with the lines.

"Yeah, I'd say they were tapped," one employee admitted after examining the professional handiwork. Someone, obviously law enforcement, wanted to illegally listen in on the private phone conversations of the Feazells. And yes, even law enforcement, to be legal, has to get court permission to legally engage in such activity. No such court authorization was ever developed.

In spite of the attempts to thwart the proceedings and because of Feazell's meticulous work, evidence was finally presented which showed that Henry Lee Lucas was a loner whose "confessions" resulted from information provided to him by law officers themselves. Those officers wanted to gain praise and notoriety from fellow law enforcement officers around the country, by helping them solve old unsolved murder cases and help them get family members of the victims off their backs, those who were pressing for the cases to be solved and someone held accountable for the murders. Henry was their "patsy". Testimony by lawmen confirmed that Lucas was frequently left in a room with files from unsolved cases. Moments later, when the drifter was questioned about the cases, he recalled their details with remarkable clarity - the mark, indeed, of a "truly credible witness."

As the grand jury's efforts continued, Vic realized that once the full effects of Lucas' bogus stories were felt, the loner would be in danger from those who had richly benefited from his tales.

Feazell had ordered Lucas to Waco, to be in his custody, at least during the grand jury. However, because of the rapidly ballooning news stories exposing the fraud across the country and the fierce reaction by some of the law officers involved, Feazell feared that Lucas might actually be killed on the return trip to Georgetown.

Vic called and pleaded for me to come down to represent Lucas and to help in the investigation. Without a moment's hesitation, I agreed. I did so without any intention of being paid for my services. It was a classic pro-bono opportunity, besides, Vic was my friend and it sounded on the phone like he was in real need of help.

Meanwhile, one by one, embarrassed officials throughout the country reopened dozens of closed cases against Lucas, and many charges were dropped as a result of Feazell's revelations. Back home, however, DPS' Adams kept spouting the party line that Lucas was indeed a mad serial killer. One example he proudly referred to was a fingerprint taken from a murder scene in Louisiana. The only problem with that bit of showmanship was that the media was already reporting that a lab had determined the print didn't belong to Lucas.

Feazell recalled the first encounter he had with Federal authorities, in the person of Assistant United States Attorney Jan Patterson. It was the spring of 1985, when he was wrapping up the third of the three Lake Waco murder cases in Cleburne, Texas. Patterson had followed him to his motel and initially attempted to befriend him.

"Let's have a drink and talk about a matter of mutual interest," the woman suggested. "Oh?" Vic responded with raised eyebrows. "And what might that be?"

Paterson hesitated, and then replied, "Lucas."

Feazell shook his head. "Nah, I'm tired. Been real busy. But it's been nice talking with you."

The Assistant U.S. Attorney grabbed him by the arm. "All right then, I'm warning you. Keep your nose out of the Lucas matter. It's none of your business."

Feazell frowned as the woman walked away. "What's going on here?" he asked himself. The more he thought about it, the more it bothered him. Patterson's surprise appearance had come barely four months after he had petitioned the Texas attorney general for a grand jury to look into Lucas' confessions. As far as he knew, Lucas hadn't been charged with a Federal crime, so why were the Feds involved ... and all so worked up? Their sudden interest in a matter outside their jurisdiction troubled him, as well it should have.

Feazell learned that a month or so earlier Patterson had also visited with state authorities at their task force headquarters in Georgetown. The group of officials concluded that, somehow, Lucas has to be spirited away from Waco where he continued to do incalculable damage to their reputations. The man's unburdening himself of his bogus confessions had to be stopped, but how? After hours of argument, it was decided that perhaps Lucas himself could be persuaded to demand to be taken back to Georgetown and out of Feazell's clutches. That job fell to a female jail minister named Clemmie Schroeder who had developed a rapport with Lucas. In truth, he had fallen madly in love with her, and other jail personnel had the impression his feelings were reciprocated, even though she was married. The group proposed that Schroeder might be able to encourage the drifter that it would be for his own good that he be returned to "safety," away from the "dangerous" Vic Feazell. One evening, Patterson sat down with Schroeder and outlined the plan. With the assistant U.S. attorney were Williamson County (Georgetown) Sheriff Jim Boutwell, Captain Bob Werner and Sergeant Bobby Prince of the Texas Rangers, and DPS chief, Colonel Jim Adams.

"We're very concerned about what's going on up in Waco," Patterson was reputed to have said. The others, especially Boutwell, chimed in with a myriad of negative statements about Vic. The sheriff was so agitated during the meeting, which lasted until midnight, that Schroeder concluded, "It was obvious he had it in for Feazell."

The rationale supporting and driving the strange session was that Feazell had kidnapped Lucas and that they were going to use the "big guns" to get him back. Finally, Boutwell boasted that "the FBI is going to go to Waco and bring Henry back." Then, in a lowered voice, he added, "You have to deal with these people a certain way."

Boutwell was true to his word. Early the next morning, FBI agents presented themselves to Feazell at the McLennan County

62

Sheriffs office and demanded to see Lucas. Vic looked at his watch: seven 0' clock, an unusually early hour for an ordinary business visit by the G-men.

"We're investigating a civil rights complaint," they told Vic as their justification to see Lucas.

"You're investigating what?" Feazell was incredulous.

"You heard right," one of the agents replied. "We want to talk to Lucas, AND NOW."

The scene struck Feazell as unreal. They're hot on a civil rights matter? The irony almost caused him to laugh.

Here was a man, Lucas, who had been ushered all around the country in the custody of law enforcement types for 18 months, had worked with them by confessing to hundreds of murder cases and related crimes, yet had rarely been represented by counsel. That little violation of his civil rights hadn't seemed to bother anyone. Now, at seven o'clock in the morning, the FBI was suddenly concerned about the handling of a man by someone who believed him to be innocent and genuinely wanted to protect his rights. Talk about hypocrisy, Feazell thought. He couldn't believe his ears.

"No way," Vic responded as he waved the agents away. "You can see him when the grand jury wraps up its questioning of him and not before."

Boutwell exploded when he learned what had happened.

"By the time we finish with Vic Feazell, he'll wish he'd never heard the name Henry Lee Lucas." Clemmie Schroeder, who was present at this outburst, didn't have any doubts as to who was included in the "we."

This was much like one of the FBI agents said to Feazell as he poked Vic in the chest and said, "You will live to regret this," before he walked away from Vic.

Boutwell was indeed talking about himself, the Texas Rangers, Jan Patterson, and the other authorities that were in on the hunt.

To Patterson, it was time for all-out war. She contacted her boss, U.S. Attorney Helen Eversberg in San Antonio. If they couldn't use traditional methods, they'd have to be "creative." Patterson asked Eversberg to subpoena Lucas to the Federal grand jury getting underway in San Antonio. Eversberg agreed. After a fight challenging the subpoena, which went all the way to the U.S.

Supreme Court, Feazell lost custody, and Henry Lee Lucas was
taken to San Antonio. But the worst was yet to come.

###

By now, it was evident to Feazell that he was the target of a
Federal grand jury probe in Austin. While he didn't know it at the
time, he was about to face the combined and seemingly
overwhelming power of the Texas Rangers, the Department of
Public Safety, the U.S. Attorney's office, the Federal Bureau of
Investigation, the Internal Revenue Service, other state law
enforcement officers, and the Waco Police Department. An
imposing array of infuriated authorities was ready to do battle
against one of their own, a man who had dedicated his life to
protecting society from those who would take advantage of others.
He wouldn't fight this battle alone, I would be by his side to the
very end.

In an example of heavy-handed harassment, the FBI had
teamed with DPS agents to unearth anything — everything — on
Vic Feazell. He soon learned that his bank records had been
subpoenaed, without appropriate legal notice, and his mail was
being opened without his knowledge or permission. From
Georgetown and Waco, the FBI and DPS broadly hinted to the
media that they were discovering extensive violations of the law
by Feazell, so they said. For months, rumors circulated that the
district attorney was very close to being indicted for serious
crimes.

The Federal-state investigation teams aggressively pursued
evidence of supposed bribes; especially those involving reduced or
dismissed drunken driving cases. They corralled anyone they could
find who had been arrested for a DWI offense in McLennan
County or who had been brought before Feazell involving such a
charge. The latter targets included lawyers, who might have been
coerced to pay off the district attorney for leniency.

"They were f-ing" rude," one exasperated man reported, "and
they threatened to reopen my case if I didn't co-operate." Another
interviewee related, "Those goons accused me of lying when I
wouldn't help them "get" Feazell."

One Waco lawyer became so incensed at the agents' high-
pressure pursuit of his clients that he drove to Austin and
confronted Jan Patterson in person.

"Get off my back!" he thundered in her face. "And leave my clients alone." He offered to undergo a polygraph test to prove he hadn't paid bribes to Feazell, but the assistant U.S. Attorney only smiled, turned, and strutted away. The frustrated lawyer said he cursed all the way home.

The vindictive juggernaut rolled on. In May of 1986, potential witnesses were called to the Federal courthouse in Waco to be quizzed about Feazell. Most of those in attendance sat uncomfortably and answered questions from Patterson, agents of the FBI and the IRS, the Waco Police Department, and numerous state law offices.

For more than a year, these agencies had aggressively searched for anything to incriminate Feazell, the enemy, a man who threatened to expose their now rapidly crumbling wild goose chase. The primary election was only weeks away, so time was against them. It was widely assumed, thanks to all the leaks by the badge-wielding pursuers, that Feazell would be indicted before then.

In addition to his favorable records in DWI cases, Feazell's office also had the highest felony conviction rate in Texas. Despite these accomplishments, Feazell was characterized at every opportunity as a "loose cannon." The law enforcement crusaders had to make their case, and fast. Lawyers were threatened with legal and tax problems if they didn't cooperate, claiming that they had taken cash from clients and had not reported it on their income for tax purposes. The authorities desperately needed incriminating evidence against the district attorney. In spite of earlier failures with attorneys, they still believed their best chance would be if they could terrify some – any local lawyers into saying that Feazell had been paid bribes for favorable decisions on DUI cases.

The going was agonizingly slow. As a matter of fact, it barely moved. Most attorneys balked at the proposals and could see, so it appeared to them, that the authorities were willing to break the law in order to get this D.A. To them, it was an obvious vendetta, the reason for which they couldn't understand. Some correctly guessed that the core of the pursuit was Feazell's revelations that Henry Lee Lucas' confessions were a hoax. The national attention, and ridicule, which had been directed at the Rangers was unforgivable to many in the law enforcement community, and it was becoming obvious to outsiders. Feazell had come a long way in making the case that Lucas was not a serial killer at all, but a serial con man.

Those who followed the matter closely realized that the cooperative effort by the authorities included the gamut of improper and illegal actions. False arrests, illegal wiretapping, improper use of individual Federal tax records, and scurrilous attempts to influence state trial and state elections - all designed to "get" Feazell by defeating him at the polls or by jailing him ... or both.

Whenever someone hesitated and courteously challenged a statement made against Vic, Patterson reportedly pointed her finger and threatened to indict the questioner. Frequently, an IRS agent would step forward and reinforce the seriousness of the threat. On occasion, an offer of immunity would be made to cap the performance. They wanted Feazell, damn it, and "cooperation" was mandatory.

To a number of the witnesses, the performance by this powerful collection of officials reeked of a bluff.

One Waco attorney was told he'd be spared from prosecution if he offered "something" on Feazell. Prosecution? The surprised man didn't realize he had been accused of anything. Even if he had, the standard procedure was for the accused to propose something in return before such a proposal was made. He replied that he didn't need their immunity. He had nothing to tell them.

"But we have to get something on Feazell," one of the interrogators stressed. "For heaven's sake, man, we'll even take gossip." It seemed that they were in a state of panic.

The yearlong pursuit of Vic Feazell was at a dead end, nothing seemed to work, and the desperate attackers were without ammunition. Yet they had to come up with something, because the May primary was drawing near.

If the normal routes wouldn't work, assistant U.S. Attorney Jan Patterson decided to meddle in local politics where the pot could be stirred more vigorously to greater effect. According to reports, Patterson had already presented the Feazell case to four Federal grand juries in Austin — all four had refused to return indictments. She realized that her last hope lay in Vic's backyard, Waco. So the day before Vic's 1986 primary, Patterson called a another grand jury into session *there* to subpoena several of Vic's friends and his administrative assistant, John Ben Sutter, who was running for county judge.

She must have promised a rewarding media show. One TV reporter was told he'd get a gratifying shot of the judicial candidate being hauled away in handcuffs. Unfortunately for the officers in waiting, no one could locate Sutter, so the show never took place. The candidate, it seems, was shaking hands miles away, and no one told him of the "photo op" he was missing.

In spite of the publicity, which was widespread and negative, Feazell won the primary, and Sutter made the runoff. Their wins were a bitter pill for the "badge" boys in pursuit. They'd been sure their attacks in the media had ruined both men in the eyes of the voters. But for Sutter, things became more and more curious. The day before the election, he had been virtually a fugitive from justice and didn't even know it. Afterwards, the FBI suddenly lost interest.

When he finally heard he was being sought, Sutter called the Bureau and offered to surrender.

"Uh, well, no need to come in," he was told. "We'll issue another subpoena later."

"Later?" Sutter frowned. "When?"

The agent couldn't be specific. In truth it was issued two weeks later, just before the June runoff election and with great fanfare. The announcement had its intended effect. Sutter lost.

At 9:30 on the morning of September 17, 1986, six weeks before the general election, Victor Fred Feazell was arrested as he ascended the steps of the McLennan County courthouse. DPS and FBI agents, slapped handcuffs over his wrists, and led him away. The scene made great television drama. Feazell raised his hands to the cameras in a defiant, thumbs-up gesture. FBI agents admitted they were upstaged by the young D.A. during the highly publicized arrest and regretted not cuffing his hands behind his back.

Feazell had been indicted and charged with violating the Hobbs Act and Federal racketeering (RICO) statutes, very serious crimes if true. From everything that I'd seen and heard, the evidence was flimsy at best, and the skimpy details of the short indictment for bribery reflected this. What neither Vic nor I knew until much later was that the grand jury which indicted Feazell was not the same grand jury which had spent a year listening to testimony that Assistant United States Attorney Patterson, had brought them. As a matter of fact, this Grand Jury had met only three times, and no witnesses had appeared before them in person. The indictment stood shakily on reports presented to them by Assistant US Attorney Patterson, and the uncorroborated testimony of two of Feazells former law partners who had desperately tried to convince Patterson of Feazells innocence but due to their on tax problems and due to threats of their being prosecuted themselves, they finally changed their story, going along with Patterson and entered into a plea bargain with Patterson and the United States Attorneys Office. Assistant US Attorney Patterson was later removed from the case because of her conduct, but that didn't stop the US Attorneys office from moving forward with all that she had done.

It turned out that Patterson, before being removed from the case, did have one more trick up her sleeve. She had obtained a warrant to search Feazell's house after his public arrest. The affidavit which was prepared in order to obtain the search warrant was rife with unsubstantiated claims and hearsay as to what the FBI expected to find: all sorts of possessions supposedly purchased with bribe money and files containing incriminating evidence. There was no basis for such expectations, but they were included for the effect they would have on local voters and, eventually, the jurors at the trial.

To cause the most damage to Feazell, and for maximum notoriety, Jan Patterson waited until the opportune moment to release the affidavit — four days before the election.

The ploy didn't work, at either level. Vic Feazell won reelection as district attorney in November, 1986, and, the following summer, a Federal court jury in Austin needed only six hours to consider five weeks of testimony from 65 government witnesses to find him innocent of all charges. In my opinion, it was a victory analogous to the Biblical story of David versus Goliath. One of the proudest moments in my career was to be standing as Vic's lawyer, shoulder to shoulder, as each of the charges were read and the words, "NOT GUILTY" followed.

Working together, Feazell and I had succeeded in conquering a seemingly overwhelming adversary, a combination of various governmental agencies devoted to his destruction and willing to use any means, legal or otherwise, to succeed in its all-consuming vendetta.

As an example of how far the authorities would go, we contended and demonstrated that the U.S. Attorney's office gave false and misleading statements to the Internal Revenue Service to gain that agency's help in the witch hunt. Indeed, we argued, the IRS's involvement was illegal.

On January 13, 1987, we obtained an affidavit from Eric V. DeLaughter, then a private investigator, but formerly a special agent with the IRS's Criminal Investigative Division. We had hired DeLaughter to interview numerous witnesses and to review various documents in preparation for the trial.

In his sworn statement, DeLaughter said that government documents, including an affidavit signed by Robert H. Zane, the main FBI agent in charge of the Feazell investigation, indicated that the probe of the district attorney was, without question, "a non-tax investigation." DeLaughter agreed and added that he could find no "bona fide basis for the IRS being involved."

"I am of the opinion that the IRS became involved in the investigation of Mr. Feazell as early as November of 1985. Records obtained from witnesses indicate the IRS was outside the scope of the grand jury investigation at that time. Records subpoenaed by the IRS include records for the year 1982 during the time when Mr. Feazell was in the private practice of law. The grand jury investigation involves allegations of Mr. Feazell in the Office of the District Attorney that did not begin until he took office in 1983. Therefore, it appears that the request of the IRS to participate in a non-tax grand jury investigation was based upon false and/or misleading information furnished to the IRS by the U.S. Attorney's office ... to gain access to a source for tax returns and tax return information that would have been unavailable to them otherwise."

DeLaughter interviewed many witnesses who told him they were directly threatened by Patterson with indictment. Others were supposedly humiliated in grueling sessions before the assistant U.S. Attorney and her team of inquisitors who, we were told, tried to get them to give adverse testimony to the grand jury regarding Feazell. In fact, DeLaughter learned later that some of the witnesses and their attorneys actually received letters that informed them that they were now targets of the Austin grand jury.

Patterson contacted one man and told him to talk to the FBI in lieu of appearing before the grand jury. The man politely told her that she subpoenaed him to testify before the grand jury and any testimony that he had to offer would be given there. This impudent affront to her authority and wishes, led to a verbal, public blistering of the witness when he later appeared in Austin to testify.

"Didn't I tell you to talk to the FBI?" she yelled at him as he entered the packed courthouse. "Didn't I?" she screamed. The man walked past her.

DeLaughter also learned that FBI and IRS agents had executed search warrants at the home of another witness. Their purpose, they informed the man as they rummaged through his belongings, was to look for evidence of gambling. However, as the exploration continued, the real reason behind the agents' assault became evident.

"Now, if you'll help us a bit," one of the agents said, "we just might be able to overlook a lot of things."

The witness was surprised and curious. "Help you? Help you in what way?"

The agents strongly suggested that if the man would furnish information concerning Vic Feazell that they would act as though the executed search warrant had not taken place and he could continue his gambling operation as usual.

"If you cooperate," he was told bluntly, "no one will ever need to know that we executed the warrant."

The witness stood mute. Had he heard what he thought he had? Well, he concluded, it was worth a try. He agreed to testify and to say something bad about Feazell.

DeLaughter later checked and found that there was no record of the warrant's being issued or served. He knew that there had been such a warrant, because he had a copy that the witness gave him. At the courthouse, U.S. magistrate Dennis Green even confirmed that he had signed it. However, all traces of the warrant, which had been issued on the sworn affidavit of Robert H. Zane, the lead FBI agent chasing Feazell, had mysteriously disappeared from official files.

###

The authorities' vendetta, their seizure by Black Robe Fever against Vic Feazell officially died with the verdict in Austin, but this appalling, extreme abuse of power was rolling with complete disregard for the law. almost from the very beginning. When it finally drew to a conclusion with Vic's complete vindication, it left behind a wretched swath of debris. Discredited assistant U.S. Attorney Jan Patterson was transferred to another jurisdiction even before the trial. Col. Jim Adams, the DPS director, resigned — and the last charge against Henry Lee Lucas was tossed out. The Internal Revenue Service, for all its inappropriate investment in manpower and resources in this ignoble affair, went away with the less-then-momentous admissions of tax evasion from two local lawyers.

A week before the start of Feazell's criminal trial in Federal Court in Austin, Texas, Federal Judge Nowlin, told us that he better not hear the name "Lucas" during the trial. "The Fifth Circuit doesn't recognize retaliation as a defense," he said.

Leaving the courthouse that day, Vic was beside himself, saying that the Judge had taken away our defense.

I asked Vic how he had done that and he responded, "He said we can't talk about Lucas and the mess surrounding him is our defense."

I asked, " Vic, what makes more sense to you? You going to prison for 84 years or me going to jail for 90 days for contempt of court?"

He responded, "You mean you're willing to do that?"

I was still bristling inside from Nowlin's charge to us, and I said, "Yes, I am, Vic. No Judge has the right to tell us how to defend your case."

The result was simple. During the first week of trial I was held in contempt of court eight times for bringing up the Lucas disaster. That Friday afternoon, Judge Nowlin told me that I would be spending my weekends in "his hotel" for violating his order not to talk about Lucas.

I responded that he, the judge, knew by now that I was willing to do that in order to see that my client got a full and fair trial, but that I would like to have a hearing before going to "his hotel" for the weekend, which he gave me. In that time, I argued that should he jail me during this lengthy trial, which turned out to be six weeks, that I was confident that any conviction would be reversed by the appellate court as I needed the weekend time with my client to prepare for trial. Moreover, I was confident that come Monday mornings that I wouldn't be in the right frame of mind to give my client what he needed and deserved. The judge relented, only a little. He assured me that I would be going to jail after the trial was over.

After Vic was completely exonerated, the judge left the bench and went to his chambers without saying a word to me about my "jail time". I went thru security, to his office, to present myself for our "unfinished" business.

The judge told me to go on home to Tulsa. He told me that he had a job to do, that I had a job to do, and that he only hoped that he did half as well at doing his job as I had done when doing mine.

Yes, I was relieved, but I had already made arrangement to be absent from society and my office for at least 90 days.

One of the funniest things that happened during the trial occurred while Vic was on the stand mentioning Lucas's name to the point that the judge finally called a recess. He ordered the attorneys and Feazell to his chambers. He angrily admonished Vic that if he said the name Lucas one more time that when the trial was over, he would put him in jail for six months for contempt of court.

Vic, in his drawn out South Texas style asked the judge if he could ask him a question? Nowlin said he could. Vic asked, "Judge, will that six months be before my 84 years or after my 84 years?" A charged room is a tough audience for really funny material!

This vendetta's claws had already reached back to Tulsa, to my personal life without me seeing the clouds gather.

When I finally arrived at home, I had an emergency call from my accountant who told me I needed to come to his office. I did so. He told me that he had received a call from the IRS unlike any he had ever received. They informed him that they had gone back 12 years on my personal tax records and that in the years '80 and '81 I had invested in tax write-off programs that they had decided to disallow and that I owed the IRS $86,000. I explained to my accountant that this was connected to the Feazell vendetta. During

Feazell's six-week trial, an IRS agent had sat in as they were trying to find any kind of tax violation on Vic. There were none. But they played havoc with me and by the time I was able to pay the assessment, with interest, etc, my bill was somewhere around $385,000. In the next Chapter, you will see how I came to be able to one day walk in to the IRS and deliver a certified check for the entire amount.

Had I worried about how Black Robe Fever infects even the agencies sworn to uphold the law and to preserve our rights —

Had I worried more about how my part in Vic's story jeopardized my finances and my career — I could never have stood up and represent my client. I would never have won a $58million verdict for Vic and he would still be in the penitentiary, at the publishing of this book.

But Vic Feazell had one more score to settle. How we settled it unfolds in the next chapter.

CHAPTER 5

WHO SAID TALK IS CHEAP?

Restoring a $58 Million Reputation

I wanted to call this chapter, "Feazell, Part II," because it presents the second and final step in the resolution of the humiliating ordeal that Vic Feazell endured as a direct result of his exposure to the Henry Lee Lucas hoax in 1985. That incident, which embarrassed and angered state law enforcement officials, among other things, led (as you read in Chapter 4) to his indictment on Federal racketeering charges the next year. Even though he was vindicated in 1987, found not guilty after a six-week trial in Federal Court in Austin, Texas where he faced 84 years if convicted, he suffered grievously. The crucifixion of Vic Feazell's personal and professional reputation had to be avenged.

It was clear to me that powerful people in high places had been terrified of this "crazy" district attorney's pursuit of the truth, and they intended to ruin him one way or the other. They decided, as one of them vowed, to "cut his legs out from under him." Fortunately, the 1987 jury in Austin had set the facts straight and set Vic free. However, what had been done to him by those who maliciously fanned the flames cried out for justice.

This chapter, therefore, is the flip side of the same seamless story, namely the disgraceful persecution of Victor Feazell. But closing the book on what Vic had been subjected to wasn't easy. It meant the patient overturning of numerous rocks to see what would crawl out. What we found led to the largest libel judgment in American history. A jury in a Civil Court in Waco, Texas would, following another six-week trial, award Vic a $58M verdict after hearing what he had endured.

###

Vic Feazell had been district attorney of McLennan County, Texas for some three years before he single handedly unraveled the sham of Henry Lee Lucas' multiple murder confessions. What had always intrigued me were the reasons for and the timing of the FBI's involvement in the state's subsequent vendetta against Vic. We were about to find out.

Working together, Federal and Texas law enforcement officials had pursued their quarry and had gotten Feazell indicted for what a jury finally decided were "trumped up" charges. Several jurors were adamant that Vic had been framed, and they said so publicly when interviewed by TV reporters the day of their verdict finding Vic not guilty. This further whetted my appetite. However, it wasn't until later that I learned that the Texas lawmen had needed to create a "public outcry" to "entice the FBI into participating" in their unjust and unseemly chase and prosecution. This they were able to do with the eager help of an investigative reporter for a Dallas television station.

While I didn't know it at the time, the arrival of Charles Duncan in 1985 was a dream-come-true for the lawmen in their developing hatchet job on Feazell. Duncan worked for WFAA, Channel 8, and with the aid of his helpful mentors on the scene and those back in Dallas, he fashioned a blistering attack on Vic's reputation. It took the form of a ten-part television series, which aired from June through August of that year. The average viewer who was not aware of the district attorney's true credibility would have concluded that Feazell was deeply involved in criminal conduct because of the way he had supposedly handled certain drunk-driving and drug-possession cases.

And that, of course, is just what happened. Following the resulting "public outcry,' he was indicted, arrested, and dragged into court. Like the Mounties, the Texas lawmen had gotten their man.

Fortunately, in 1987, Vic was acquitted of all federal charges following a highly publicized six-week trial. He resigned as district attorney the next year, after staying on for 18 months at his wife's insistence. But the next battle was just beginning. Feazell had crossed the Ozarks; the Rockies lay ahead.

###

In June of 1986, a year after the television series began and one day before the statute of limitations would have barred litigation, Vic filed a $58M civil libel suit against A.H. Belo Corporation, Belo Broadcasting Corporation (WFAA), and investigative reporter Charles Duncan. I don't think he really had any thoughts of pursuing the case at the time, especially since he was preoccupied with his reelection campaign and worse, was under the investigation that ultimately led to his indictment. Also weighing heavily on his mind was the knowledge that he was the target of a Federal grand jury probe. However, Vic wanted to protect his rights for later.

"Later" came the next year, shortly after he was acquitted of the criminal charges in Austin. Vic telephoned me.

"Gary, the Belo lawyers called today. They want to take depositions in my defamation lawsuit against them."

Feazell had been through hell in handcuffs, and I knew what he was thinking. He didn't relish more years in the courtroom, under relentless and very public scrutiny. His family didn't either. But it was fish-or-cut-bait time. The choice was either to let them take their depositions or to drop the case. Put another way, he could reopen old wounds, with the goal being ultimate closure, or he could walk away, in peace, temporary peace, perhaps. We talked for a few minutes.

"Let's let them take some depositions," I finally suggested, "and let's see what happens." I added that since, at the time, I didn't know anything about defamation lawsuits, the depositions might be enlightening. "If we don't turn up anything helpful along the way," I reflected, "we can always dismiss the suit. " What turned out to be the single largest defamation case in US history, was that close to being voluntarily dismissed *by the plaintiff*, Vic.

But finally, Vic agreed. The Belo lawyers began the discovery process.

Curiously, the next biggest challenge I had with Vic was to get him to amend his pleadings to allege that he never would have been indicted but for the television series. I knew he'd always felt that way in his heart, but his head - and his anger - had been focused on the Texas Rangers and the other lawmen that had gone after him with a vengeance.

"Vic, you have to do it. If we're going to go to trial, we have to make that change in your pleadings. It's crazy to proceed without it. Without question, Belo defamed you, but I think we can establish that you never would have been *indicted* without their active participation with the authorities."

There was no question in my mind: Belo's television series had produced the public outcry that brought in the FBI and led to Feazell's indictment. The lawmen couldn't find an informant, since there was nothing to inform on, so they had to create a public outcry. It was classic FBI 101. They desperately needed Charles Duncan, and he did his job admirably.

"It was bad enough that they ruined your reputation, but, by accommodating and forwarding the vendetta all the way to the courthouse, what WFAA did was to blow everything into the realm of absolute fantasy," I told Feazell.

"A nightmare, Gary," Vic replied calmly, "an absolute nightmare." He hesitated for a second. "Let's make that amendment."

Over the next few weeks, the further the Dallas lawyers went with their questioning, the more interesting things looked for us. Once we started deposing Duncan, we spotted numerous holes, untruths, and cover-ups. I realized then that we indeed had a case, potentially a major one.

###

Vic Feazell's defamation suit against A.H. Belo Corporation, Belo Broadcasting Corporation, and Charles Duncan got underway in Waco's 19 Judicial District Court at 10 a.m. on Monday, March 11, 1991, before a jury of nine men and three women. Visiting Judge James R. Meyers of Austin presided. Belo's lawyers were John McElhaney and Tom Leatherbury of the 180-member Dallas law firm of Locke, Purnell, Rain, and Harrell.

I intended to prove that Charles Duncan was a tool of the lawmen in their vendetta, that it was his 10-part television series on WFAA, which ignited the firestorm intended to consume my client, and that Belo and Duncan were guilty of actual malice. We called Duncan as our fist witness. He was on the stand for eleven days under a grueling and enlightening cross examination, one that I had spent days preparing. It was, to me, like a championship-boxing match.

Charles Duncan came to Waco in April of 1985 and got right to work. He made all the proper contacts, if you know what I mean. (Among other things, he was even allowed to store his files in a safe at the Federal Building.) While the defendants stoutly maintained that the official investigation of Feazell began before Duncan's series aired, the reporter yielded under questioning and told part of the truth. He said he'd once informed the state board, which licenses private investigators, that "after I began my investigation, a joint federal-state-city investigation began, resulting in the indictment of the D.A."

He left out the part about the television series. The complete sequence was (1) Duncan started his investigation, (2) WFAA aired his 10-part series, (3) the authorities began their investigation, and (4) the indictment was handed down in Austin.

The story that Duncan "created", which followed his preconceived opinion, was vicious, devastating, and above all — untrue. It portrayed Feazell as a corrupt district attorney who had taken bribes from Waco lawyers in return for dismissing charges, particularly DWI offenses, and otherwise given favorable treatment to their clients. Low morale in the police department was blamed on his lax prosecution. The series reported that the FBI was investigating this sinister D.A., or was about to.

It was clear to us that the multi-part television program was designed to captivate and assist the FBI to jump into the Feazell matter. After all, someone this bad had to be investigated. Isn't that what the FBI is supposed to do under such circumstances? It was a clever, malicious attempt to destroy Vic Feazell's reputation and ability to make a living, and it nearly did, but it backfired. It ended up making Vic and me multi-millionaires.

We also learned that the government had prepared a psychological report on Vic. It concluded that he would commit suicide under all of this pressure, so he'd never be around to face the charges and be able to defend them.

In his testimony, Duncan stood by his statements. However, his tale quickly unraveled when we presented numerous witnesses who flatly contradicted what the reporter had sworn they'd said. Dean Priddy, a former sergeant in the Waco Police Department's Drug Enforcement Unit, stated that Duncan sought only negative information about Feazell during a 1985 interview with Waco police agents. Priddy said that Duncan was "out to do what he could to discredit" the district attorney. In addition, the former Waco police chief testified that Duncan had taken his remarks out of context. We then presented a WFAA script that accused Vic of joining the police department to avoid the draft. The only problem with that allegation was that Vic wasn't old enough at the time to be drafted.

On the stand, Feazell was adamant that Duncan's unfounded and savage tale, created the basis for the FBI to open its "official" investigation. Without a doubt, that was what ultimately led to Vic's indictment in September of 1986. When McElhaney asked Vic if he were paranoid, he laughed. "You know the saying. 'You're not really paranoid if they really are out to get you.'"

One of the key operatives behind the initiation of the official vendetta was a smug jurist who despised Feazell. His named was Walter S. Smith, Jr.

Then-Texas Governor Bill Clements appointed Smith to the state bench in 1980. Smith then lost a 1982 reelection bid, during which Vic campaigned for his winning opponent, Judge Allen. Over the years, Smith ran for office twice and lost twice in McLennan County. He became a U.S. District Judge in Waco on October 6, 1984. Smith had tried only two Federal cases before becoming a Federal Judge. Both were civil cases while he was a U.S. Magistrate.

Judge Smith inserted himself into this civil case, even while he sat on the bench in Federal Court, to testify on behalf of the Belo defense against Vic's character. He was their only "live" witness. They had others, including two more judges, but after my cross examination of Judge Walter Smith, the other two judges exited the Court House, and the defense decided not to bring any more witnesses to testify.

There was no doubt that Smith hated Feazell. On direct examination, he growled, "His reputation was that of a district attorney who was on 'the take.'" When asked by John McElhaney if he had an opinion as to Vic's reputation for truth and veracity, Smith responded quickly, "I do. It's bad." To me, on cross-examination, he added, "I haven't had any respect for Mr. Feazell for some time." That was an understatement. But Smith hadn't kept his animosity to himself. He combined his feelings with vindictive action.

Smith insisted his negative opinion of Vic stemmed from late September or early October of 1984, predating the WFAA television series. That was when, he said, David Hodges, a county court-at-law judge in Waco, came to visit him in the U.S. magistrate's office to deliver some "truths" about Feazell. Smith said he merely directed Hodges to the FBI, whose office was down the hall. He added that he also talked with "a couple of lawyers" about Vic, then sent a memo to Jan Patterson, the Assistant U.S. Attorney in Austin who handled the Waco criminal docket.

He wanted to make her aware of what he had heard and that she should listen to the lawyers he had talked to.

Judge Smith admitted the TV series had a detrimental impact on what was left of Feazell's reputation. He breezily went on to say that just because Vic had been acquitted in Austin didn't necessarily mean he was innocent. It's just that the jury "could not make the finding beyond a reasonable doubt." I couldn't believe my ears. That jury was in the absolute best position to decide Vic's guilt or innocence, and I told him so. As a matter of fact, I pointed out that five Austin jurors had said it was likely that Vic was framed by law enforcement with the help of the Belo Corporation.

Smith had been quite busy before Feazell's indictment. Among other activities, he'd driven to San Antonio to meet with U.S. Attorney Helen Eversberg, "in order to serve justice." He told her she needed to do something; either present the case to the grand jury or announce to the world that the investigation was over with and there would be no prosecution of Mr. Feazell. It was a not-so-subtle hint to get on with the show. **At the end of this chapter, see excerpts from the Smith cross-examination.**

I had no doubt that the FBI wasn't investigating Vic in 1984, before Duncan's television series. I asked Smith if he knew that the first time Judge Hodges met with the FBI he met with Special Agent Robert H. Zane and DPS investigator Ronald E. Boyter together. Smith said he wasn't aware of that.

I raised an eyebrow. "Wasn't it in 1985?"

"No."

When the FBI initiates an investigation, it opens a file. Ron Boyter clearly remembered that in Vic's case, the first discussion with the FBI was on April 26, 1985. Not 1984. And Boyter denied in a deposition that he told Duncan anything about any investigation in April, because one had not been started at that time. Also, curiously, no one else had heard the rumors in 1984 that Judge Smith claimed he had heard, which had led to a negative opinion.

The truth is, there were no rumors whatsoever about Vic in the initial FBI files, just the Lucas matter.

But there was a lot about Feazell, which Judge Smith had wanted included in the FBI files. In 1985, his then wife Jill Allen received an anonymous letter, which briefed her on Smith's "extracurricular activities." That letter had initially gone to his neighbor, Richard Franks, whose son was one of the three young people killed in the Lake Waco murders. Smith, using obscenities, informed Franks that the FBI had told him that Berni Feazell, Vic's wife, was probably responsible for the letter. Smith also told Franks not to let Feazell prosecute his son's murder case because, in his opinion, the D.A. was incompetent. His solution? Franks should hire one of Smith's former law associates to do the job as a special prosecutor.

Federal District Judge James R. Nowlin disclosed that Smith was often in his chambers during Feazell's criminal trial in Austin. Nowlin admitted he'd never seen a judge get so involved in another judge's case. Smith had also talked with witnesses there. He even took the wife of one of them to visit Judge Nowlin.

But there was more. Someone fired a gun at Judge Smith one day while he was jogging. As in any attack on a Federal judge, the FBI investigated. Because of what Smith told them, Feazell became a suspect of the shooting and was questioned about it. Later Smith received telephone threats. Again, Feazell was a suspect. However, the FBI quickly shut down the investigations when the agency learned that these occurrences "had something to do with Smith's personal life."

Judge Smith attended a meeting in Jan Patterson's office in July of 1985 during which he presented to her and FBI special agent, Bob Zane, an envelope containing two one-page typewritten letters. The messages inside were innocuous and had nothing to do with Vic, yet the FBI made them a part of his file after Smith claimed Vic had written them. Afterwards, typewriters were seized from Vic's home, and typewriter balls were removed from the district attorney's office. Fingerprints, too, were checked. Nothing matched.

###

Once, after entering private practice, Feazell filed a *pro hac vice* motion in Judge Smith's court, so he could represent a client without being formally admitted. Typically, such a motion is commonly and quickly approved. However, Smith denied

Feazell's application without a hearing of any kind. The judge said he'd denied maybe two others in his career. Those, unlike Vic's, were for good cause. It was obvious he singled out Vic for special treatment- an immediate thumbs down. Vic wanted to file a motion to have Smith recuse himself because of prejudice so another Federal judge could handle the case. However, because Feazell couldn't act under a *pro hac vice* motion, he couldn't even make that request himself.

Then there was the 1988 letter that Judge Smith wrote to Ben Selman, the chairman of the District 86 Grievance Committee. It concerned a case in Sherman, Texas, in which Smith was not involved, but he felt his two cents would be worth a lot. Feazell had been placed on probation for a year, during which time he was not to violate the canon of ethics. But because of Vic's comments after a judge had barred the media and gallery from hearing certain testimony in a jury trial, Smith saw an opportunity to trash his nemesis again. Vic had complained publicly that such action was unconstitutional. He did use some unconventional language in making his point, but he was correct in his assessment of the First Amendment's protections. A sheriff was testifying, not some confidential informant, as Smith wrote to Selman. Obviously, Smith's letter was a blatant attempt to have Feazell's license revoked. After considering the particulars, the Grievance Committee refused to take any action.

Judge Walter S. Smith, Jr. was the last witness. The defense rested on Tuesday afternoon, April 16. We rested after briefly recalling Duncan and Feazell as rebuttal witnesses and playing a December, 1985, episode of *60 Minutes*, which featured Vic and Henry Lee Lucas.

The Waco jurors had heard nearly six weeks of testimony. We spent most of Wednesday hammering out the court's charges to the jury, and both sides made their closing statements on Thursday, April 18. The jury retired to deliberate immediately afterwards.

In March, we had offered to settle for $3 million. I told the defense that our offer would increase by $1 million each Monday throughout the trial. I cautioned, however, that once the case went to the jury, the offer would be void. The lawyers for WFAA and Duncan laughingly rejected our proposal. By the time the jury retired that Thursday, the settlement offer had climbed to $8 million.

Shortly after the jury returned with its verdict, Feazell was gracious. "I have a very special thanks for 24 special people- the twelve in Austin who found me not guilty in 1987 and the twelve here today."

On Friday, April 19, the jury returned. It had taken them just over two hours to reach their verdict. They delivered incredible news: Feazell was entitled to $58 million, the largest libel award in U.S. history. Of this, $2 million was for damage to his business, $9 million for damage to his reputation, $6 million for humiliation and mental suffering, $40 million in exemplary damages from Belo, and $1 million in exemplary damages from Duncan.

When it was over, the defendants' attorneys dashed away in silence. As Vic left the courtroom, he stopped and faced reporters." I want to thank God. God led us, God preserved us, and God gave us this victory."

Later, sitting in Vic's living room, I looked at a painting of Texas bluebonnets that hung on the wall. It was a faithful representation of the usually peaceful landscape around Waco. I hadn't noticed it before. We called this part of his home our "command bunker" during the trial. Now it was our brief refuge from a brutal war, which we had won. I reflected not only over the past six weeks but also on the years Vic and I had faced the seemingly overwhelming forces of abuse from a law enforcement community and its allies on a rampage.

The jury wasn't always with us. They told us at a party we held for them the night of the verdict that at the start of the trial they had heard so much that they couldn't see how we could overcome the rumor mill, which had been created against Vic. They had seen Charles Duncan's series on TV, and it had seemed so believable. But, fortunately and step by step, we were able to overcome all of their hesitations. I talked to them just the way I would converse with my mother and dad, sitting around the kitchen table. I never talked down to them ... just to them. One of the lawyers on the other side made a major mistake during his opening statement when he loftily informed the jurors that he and his co-counsel would be using a lot of big words in the trial and that he hoped that they could somehow comprehend.

The defense never recovered from that arrogant crack.

I've always said that as an advocate for a client one should never be friendly with the lawyers on the other side in the presence of the jury. Early on I told Vic that, in my opinion, the jury would not like the defense attorneys, so I was going to do a number of things to convey to them that I didn't like the lawyers either. As a matter of fact, a number of jurors later told us they were so turned off by the defense's testimony and the way the Belo and Duncan attorneys handled the case that they would have returned a verdict of $100 million, if we'd just asked!

As for Judge Walter S. Smith, Jr., we proved that he lied to the men and women of the jury in trying to convince them that Vic's problems started before the Lucas matter came to surface. The evidence showed that to be an absolute lie. Its whole purpose was to create a public outcry.

This case was Vic Feazell's revenge. Had I been responsible for developing the lawsuit, I probably never would have proceeded. As I mentioned earlier, I didn't know anything about defamation litigation before we started. Lawyers say such actions are long shots and that you can't be successful at them. But I learned quickly, I presented the facts fairly, and my client was vindicated. And Vic Feazell was a good client. He really allowed me to direct the case, and he had total confidence in my decisions.

Judge James R. Meyers was a fair judge, an excellent judge. It was pure pleasure to try this matter in his courtroom.

I know the Belo lawyers never dreamed that they were going to get popped the way they did. They had offered us $75,000 early on, then two weeks before trial they increased the amount to $500,000. Three or four days before we went to court, they boosted the ante to $700,000. That was as far as they would go. They thought we were crazy when we started at $3 million, then increased the sum by $1 million each week.

The message of this case? Keep plugging and never give up. Justice will most often prevail if you stay in there, committed to your cause. The little guy can overcome the entrenched power structure, even if, as in out situation, the other side spends ten times the money. They laughed at us most of the way, but the jury saw the truth of the tragedy that had happened to Vic, and set things right. A final note: But for certain law enforcement types who tried to ruin Vic Feazell, none of this would have happened. It's a tragedy that an innocent man was subjected to such abuse, but he persevered and prevailed.

PARTS OF THE CROSS EXAMINATION

OF US FEDERAL JUDGE WALTER SMITH:

Judge Smith was quite prejudiced towards Vic Feazell as Vic had supported Judge Smith's opponent when Judge Smith ran for re-election for the State Court bench and the candidate that Vic supported beat him. During the cross examination this exchange took place.

Q: (Richardson questioning Federal Judge Walter Smith). Have you ever had a jury return a not guilty verdict, Judge, and then tell the media that in their opinion the defendant had been framed?

A: No, I haven't.

Q: As a matter of fact, myself as a former U.S. attorney and yourself as a federal judge, have you ever heard of that happening before?

A: Oh, yes, I've heard of it. It doesn't happen real often.

Q: It's a real rarity. Would you agree?

A: Doesn't happen often.

Q: Do you know that that's what the folks down in Austin told the media, five of them, that in their opinion, who saw the evidence, who heard the evidence, who evaluated the witnesses, concluded that there was an effort made to frame Vic Feazell?

A: No, sir, I don't know that.

Q: You never read that article right here in the *Waco Tribune-Herald*?

A: I may have read it in the Waco paper. That doesn't mean I know it.

Note: Even Federal Judges try to get cute when being cross-examined.

Q: Well, you know that they told the reporter that, don't you?

A: No, sir, I don't know that.

Q: Were you the Federal Judge that signed orders for a wiretap on Vic Feazell's home?

A: I know of nothing about any wiretap of Vic Feazell's home, ever.

Q: Judge, would you say that you get along real well with the big boys, but you don't fair too well with the voting people?

A: No, sir, I wouldn't say that.

Q: Well, let's see. You were appointed to the bench in 1980. Who appointed you?

A: Bill Clemmons (Texas Governor).

Q: And then you ran for re-election in '82?

A: Yes, sir.

Q: And the voters didn't re-elect you, did they?

A: They did not.

Q: And Vic Feazell campaigned vigorously for Judge Allen, didn't he?

A: I don't know that. *(He knew it)*

Q: You say you don't know that Vic Feazell put his organization behind Judge Allen?

A: No, sir, I didn't know that. That's news to me.

Note: everyone in the courtroom knew he was lying.

Q: And then, Judge, you were appointed then — how many times did you run for office?

A: Twice.

Q: How many times did you win?

A: I haven't won, yet.

Q: And both of them here in this community, right?

A: Yes.

Q: So then you didn't win the second time either, and shortly after that you got another appointment, didn't you?

A: Yes, in October, 1984.

Q: And who appointed you to the bench that time?

A: President Reagan.

Q: Are you getting an idea of where we would be today if it weren't for your connections with the "big guys" and you had to depend on the voters for your future?

A: (no answer)

Q: Judge, you've had what we could classify as a fairly hostile attitude toward Vic Feazell for sometime, haven't you?

A: I don't know if that's the word I would use. I haven't had any respect for Mr. Feazell for sometime. I haven't had any occasion to be hostile. I don't personally know the man. We haven't had any personal contact.

Q: Well Judge, do you remember back in 1985 when your then wife, Jill Allen, received an anonymous letter that was telling her about your sexual escapades. Do you remember that letter?

Mr. Leatherbury: (defense counsel) Your Honor, this is the matter that he had been instructed to come to the bench about.

The Court: Come up.

(Discussion off record at the bench.)

By Mr. Richardson:

Q: Judge Smith, do you remember back in 1985 receiving a letter that initially went to the home of your neighbor, Richard Franks, and that when brought to you, to your wife, an anonymous letter addressing matters pertaining to your personal life?

A: I don't remember the part about it originally going to my neighbor, but certainly I remember that letter.

Q: Do you remember taking the position that it was your opinion that Vic Feazell was behind the letter coming to your wife?

A: No, sir. I don't think I ever took that position.

Q: You don't think so?

A: Not that I recall. If you want me to explain that, I will.

Q: What about — did you take the position that Vic Feazell or his wife, or someone that had something to do with them, was behind that letter?

A: I was told that Bernie Feazell (Vic's wife) probably was responsible for that letter, yes, sir.

Q: Who told you that?

A: The FBI.

Q: Well, Judge, they took that letter—isn't that the letter that they took and took fingerprints of Mr. Frank's fingerprints were on that letter?

A: I don't know.

Note: Mr. Franks was the next-door neighbor to whom the letter mistakenly went to by the postal service.

Q: And they also brought Mrs. Feazell over there after Vic was arrested, and took her fingerprints, didn't they?

A: I don't know.

Note: He knew.

Q: And you know they took Mr. Feazell's fingerprints, don't you?

A: That's standard when anybody's arrested.

Q: Right. So I take it then, you had the FBI to fingerprint – take fingerprints off this correspondence?

A: I did not have the FBI do anything, Counselor.

Q: Okay. So no fingerprints were taken off of it?

A: I gave them the letter as I am requested to do, whenever I get any kind of letter like that.

Note: Not!!! There is no way, in my opinion, this Judge would have given this letter to the FBI unless he thought he could tie it to the Feazells. As a former United States Attorney, myself, I am convinced of this.

Q: Now Richard Franks is your neighbor, is he not?

A: Yes, sir.

Q: He has known you since 1980, hasn't he?

Note: we had done our homework.

A: Before that, yes, sir.

Q: Ya'll (Texas slang by Richardson who grew up in deep South Texas) have lived next door to each other or lived in the same complex since 1980?

A: He lives behind me, yes sir.

Q: You all swim in the same community swimming pool?

A: Maybe twice in 12 years, yes sir.

Q: Okay. Do you remember, Judge, when Mr. Frank's son was one of the three killed out here that became known as the Lake Waco murder matter?

Note: Vic Feazell prosecuted, successfully, those involved in killing Mr. Frank's son and due to his appreciation for what Vic did, and his admiration of Vic as a prosecutor, Mr. Franks brought this information to us.

A: Vividly.

Q: Do you remember advising Mr. Franks that he should not let Vic Feazell prosecute the case because Vic Feazell was incompetent?

A: No sir, I don't remember that.

Q: Are you saying you didn't tell him that?

A: I can't imagine that I did.

Q: Do you remember encouraging him, instead, to go hire a special prosecutor, to-wit, one of your former law associates?

A: No sir.

Q: Do you remember using obscenities to Richard Franks in describing your opinion of Vic Feazell?

A: No sir.

Q: Do you deny it?

A: I don't have any memory about what you're talking about, Mr. Richardson.

Note: As you can see, even Federal Judges can conveniently have a lapse of memory.

Q: My question is, do you deny it? Do you deny using obscenities back in 1983, do you deny using – or '84, that time period, do you deny using obscenities?

A: Can't deny or admit it. I have no memory at all.

Note: You are learning from this, that those know the parameters can always use this one in the courtroom. "I have memory at all".

Q: Let me finish. Do you deny using obscenities when talking to Richard Franks about your attitude toward Vic Feazell? In 1983 or '84, in that time period?

A: I can't admit or deny that because I don't have any memory of it.

Q: Okay. Judge, talking about your quote getting along with the power structure, I guess, is a good way to put it, you remember the case of police officer <u>Mike Nicoletti vs. City of Waco</u>?

A: Yes sir.

Q: There was one point four million dollar ($1.4 million dollar) verdict in that case, wasn't there?

Mr. McElhaney: (another defense lawyer) Your Honor, this is entirely extraneous (not relevant): in fact, was excluded from evidence before. We move to strike as being immaterial and irrelevant.

The Court: Come up.

(Discussion off record between the Court and Counsel)

Cross continued by Mr. Richardson:

Q: Judge, let me ask you---

Mr. McElhaney: Your Honor, could the ruling be on the record that we move to---

The Court: Well, the objection was not on the record, but the objection made at the bench was sustained. We can make a record of it at a recess.

Q: Let me ask you, Judge, if you've been known to occasionally, when a large verdict is against, lets say, the power structure, to reverse that verdict?

Mr. McElhaney: Your Honor, we object on the grounds that this is immaterial, and it doesn't involve Mr. Feazell at all.

The Court: And I sustained the objection.

Cross-examination continued by Mr. Richardson:

Q: When you were appointed a Federal Judge, what was your experience in Federal Court at that time?

A: Mr. Richardson, I had to fill out a form that was probably 25-30 pages long. I don't remember, I didn't have a large number of trials in Federal court if that's what you're asking.

Q: Well, what I'm trying to find out is, had you tried any cases in Federal Court before you became Federal Judge?

A: Yes sir.

Q: Several or –

A: Two as I recall at the moment.

Q: Two?

A: Yes sir.

Q: What kind of cases were those?

Note: The reason I am asking these questions is because, as you will see, Judge Walter Smith had very little experience in Federal Court and yet he denied Vic Feazell the right to get admission to the Federal Court, even with all of Vic's experience and yet he wants to continue to represent that he is not hostile to Vic.

A: A products liability case against Ford Motor Company, and an anti-trust case involving Snelling and Snelling Employment Agency are the two I recall.

Q: And both of those were civil case; is that correct?

A: Yes sir.

Q: And that was the entirety then of your Federal Court experience before you were appointed to the bench as Federal Judge?

A: No sir.

Q: As far as---

A: Those were the two trials I recall. There were other matters that didn't result in trial. I defended a bank robber one time, but it was a guilty plea.

Q: Let me hand you, Judge, what has been marked as Plaintiffs Exhibit 138 and ask you to take a moment, please, and look at that.

A: Yes sir.

Q: Tell me if you are familiar with it?

A: Yes sir. I recognize it as a motion filed in the Waco Division of the Federal District Court.

Q: Judge, Vic Feazell, after he was District Attorney and resigned and became employed in the community with a company here, ASK, filed a motion in your courtroom asking permission---well, he filed a *pro hac vice* motion did he not?

Note: *this is when a lawyer is not admitted to a Court and asks permission to come into the Court for just the one case. In all of my years as an attorney, I have seen many such requests by attorneys and this is the only one I have ever seen denied.*

A: He has done that more than once.

Q: Well, I'm talking about in this particular instance. We'll deal with all of them, but he's filed a *pro hac vice* motion in your court, has he not?

A: Yes sir.

Q: Basically what that is saying, Judge, could I come
   into your courtroom and handle a lawsuit; isn't that
   basically — handle this particular lawsuit, and not
   just come in, but, could I come into your courtroom
   and handle this particular lawsuit?

A: When a lawyer is not licensed to practice in the
   court, yes sir.

Q: And being licensed to practice, for example, in the
   Federal Court is tantamount to filling out a form
   and paying a fee, is it not?

A: No sir.

Q: Well, different jurisdictions have different
   requirements. What are the requirements in the
   Western District?

Note: This is the District Judge Smith worked in.

A: You have to either complete an approved six-eight
   hour seminar or pass the written examination.

Q: Okay, and it's all—it is common, is it not, for
   lawyers who have not yet been licensed, for
   example, in a particular Federal District to file a
   motion called *pro hac vice*?

A: It is.

Q: And it's extremely common for Judges to just
   arbitrarily approve those, is it not?

A: I'm not sure about arbitrarily, but they are commonly
   approved, yes sir.

Q: How many such lawyers would you say, Judge, since
   you have been on the Federal bench that you have
   denied the right to come into your courtroom on a
   particular case when they've filed a motion *pro hac
   vice*?

A: Probably a dozen.

Note: I say, NO WAY.

Q: Twelve?

A: Yes sir. That would be a guess.

Note: Another lesson. When a witness says he/she is guessing, that lets them off the hook, so to speak.

Q: And Vic Feazell is one of those lawyers, isn't he?

A: Yes sir.

Q: And what are some of the reasons why you, for example, deny *pro hac vice?*

A: In his case or just in general?

Q: Just in general.

A: The others that I remember are situations where a lawyer is admitted to practice in a case and a condition of that admittance is that they go ahead and get themselves admitted generally within a certain period of time and when they don't do that, they just keep coming back and seeking *pro hac vice* status and they don't agree to that.

Q: Then let me rephrase it. Had Vic Feazell, prior to the case that you have before you there, <u>James Randel vs. American Solar King</u> and Brian B. Pardo, had Vic Feazell ever before that submitted a *pro hac vice* request in your courtroom?

A: I don't recall. I don't think so.

Q: And you denied it on this particular case, didn't you?

A: I believe so, yes sir.

Note: He knows so.

Q: Tell me how many other lawyers, Judge, that you have denied a request for pro hac vice when they asked for it on the first occasion?

A: Maybe two.

Q: Do you remember the circumstances of those?

A: They were very young lawyers who worked for a government agency and there were like already two or three lawyers who were representing that government agency and we just decided that agency didn't need five lawyers representing it in one case, so we just said, no.

Q: Would you agree Judge that you more or less singled out Vic Feazell by refusing him a *pro hac vice* in this case?

A: No sir. He's the only lawyer who ever applied during a period when his license was on probation.

Q: Well, Judge, are you – you realize that Mr. Feazell had been accepted, the time that he made his request to your courtroom, he had been accepted in the Federal US Bankruptcy Court; did you not?

A: Did I realize that?

Q: Yes sir.

A: If that's — probably yes. I don't recall now.

Q: You also knew, Judge, did you not, that he had been accepted while he was on probation to the Southern Federal District up in Dallas at the time that you refused to let him come to your Courtroom and handle a civil lawsuit; did you not?

A: That may be. I don't recall.

Q: Would you say, Judge, that the appearance of singling out a lawyer and retaliating against him?

A: No sir.

Q: Judge, one of the things you cited in your refusal to allow Vic Feazell to come into your courtroom was that he didn't have enough experience in the Federal Court system; is that not correct?

A: I don't know sir. Is that order part of this exhibit, Mr. Richardson?

Q: No, your order is not a part of it. But look at page 5 of that motion, top motion.

A: Yes sir.

Q: Item number 10. On the same date, October 20, 1988, this Court – this said Court denied defendant's general counsel motion to appear *pro hac vice* noting that applicant, quote, "has no experience in Federal Court." That was one of the reasons you stated; was it not?

A: That's what this says, if that's what you're asking me.

Q: Do you know of any reason to believe that this isn't correct?

A: No sir.

Q: Filed in your Courtroom, right? Because it's a motion to recuse you; is it not?

A: Yes sir.

Q: What is a motion to recuse, or for recusal?

A: A motion requesting the particular judge before which a case is pending to step down and allow another Judge to hear the matter.

Q: That was a motion that was filed by Mr. Feazell; was it not? Asking you to step down as a Federal Judge and let some other Judge deal with his *pro hac vice* and handle the case?

A: This was signed by Brian Pardo, pro se.

Q: Well, it's Mr. Prado attempting to recuse you based on allegations that you have a great deal of prejudice toward Vic Feazell; does it not?

A: I don't really recall what his reasons were.

Q: You would agree, would you not, that Mr. Feazell couldn't even file his motion in your court since you wouldn't allow him *pro hac* status?

A: Yes sir.

Q: Judge, during the time that you were – that Vic
    Feazell was on trial down in Austin, Texas (Vic's
    criminal trial) would you agree that you were in
    Austin and even in Judge Nowlin's (the trial judge
    in Vic's criminal trial) chambers on a reasonably
    regular basis during Vic's trial in Austin?

A: I go to Austin the third full week of every month,
    I'm sure I was there during that week unless for
    some reason it was changed to another week, yes
    sir.

Q: Are you aware that Judge Nowlin said that he had
    never seen a judge get so involved in another
    judge's case?

A: No sir, I'm sure not. I doubt that he said that, Mr.
    Richardson.

Q: You doubt that he said that?

A: Yes sir, I do.

Q: Well, let me ask you this in that regard. You were
    out in the hall rather frequently, talking to witnesses
    that, for example, Don Hall's wife (Mr. Hall was
    one of the Waco lawyers that was brow beaten by
    law enforcement to testify against Vic), you took
    her in to visit Judge Nowlin, didn't you?

A: Not that I recall. (Wow. Anyone believe this?)

Q: Or at least into Judge Nowlin's chambers, past the
    locked door?

A: Don Hall's wife?

Q: Yes sir.

A: I don't recall – I wouldn't know Don Hall's wife if she walked in the door.

Q: You know Don Hall?

A: Yes sir, I know Don Hall. I visited with Don Hall, but I don't recall visiting with his wife at all.

Q: You remember the lady that was with him when he was down there to testify?

A: When I chatted with Don Hall he was by himself in a little anteroom of some kind there on the second floor of the Federal Courthouse in Austin.

Q: Was that before he took the stand, Judge?

A: I don't know.

Q: Judge, in the retrieval of FBI files that we were able to get in this case, there were some — quite a few — there were some matters that we asked just for FBI files pertaining to Vic Feazell under the fortieth request, do you know how it ended up in Vic Feazell's file, the matter pertaining to someone shooting at you while you were jogging one day?

A: I have no idea how that would be in Vic Feazell's file.

Q: Would it mean that maybe they were investigating Vic Feazell to see if he shot at you?

A: I doubt it. I have no idea.

Q: Do you know, Judge, how in May of '85 there was – why there was a memo developed pertaining to the investigation of Vic Feazell involving phone threats that you claimed that you'd received?

A: I have no idea what you're talking about, Mr. Richardson.

Q: Well, did you report that you had received some phone threats back in May of '85?

A: I could well have. Unfortunately that happens from time to time. I don't recall any particular dates.

Q: Do you have any idea how an FBI file would show up – note memos – would show up in Vic Feazell's file that had to do with phone threats that you claimed that you received in May of '85?

A: I have no idea.

Q: Let me hand you Plaintiff's exhibit # 139, Judge, documents that came out of the Department of Public Safety records that we got under the document request records, and ask you, if you would, please look at that and see if that's the document that on May the 10th, 1985, documents that deal with allegations that someone shot at you on May 8th, '85.

A: No sir; I don't read it that way.

Q: This deals with a different matter. This is the phone threat that I asked you about. This deals with the phone threats. About someone buying a gun, does it not?

A: Yes sir.

Q: Okay. Judge, have you had a chance to read the document?

A: Yes sir. I remember more about this now.

Q: Do you have any idea how this matter would end up in Vic Feazells investigative file with the Department of Public Safety?

A: I do not.

Q: Did you give them any reason to believe that Vic Feazell had anything to do with this matter?

A: I did not.

Q: You mentioned – you were shot at while you were jogging one day, didn't you?

A: Yes sir.

Q: And the FBI started an investigation on this, didn't they?

A: Started it? Yes sir.

Q: Yes sir. And didn't they quickly shut it down? Do you remember what they learned?

A: They didn't quickly shut it down. It lasted for some period of time.

Q: Okay. Did they learn whether or not it had something to do with your personal life, Judge?

A: As far as I know, it did not.

Q: My question is, did they learn that it had something to do with your personal life?

A: No sir. They did not learn that. It had something to do with a gentleman I had sentenced as a State judge.

Q: Who was that?

A: Wilford Padilla.

Q: Did they ever bring charges against him for shooting at you judge?

A: No sir.

Q: That would be rather strange, wouldn't it, if they thought they had evidence on somebody for shooting at a Federal judge and they didn't charge them with it?

Mr. McElhaney: Objection, your Honor.

Q: Let me ask you this way. Wouldn't that be the normal thing to do if the FBI thought they had information linking to this Padilla fellow---?

Mr. McElhaney: Objection

Q: Judge, let me hand you Plaintiff's Exhibit # 140 and ask you to take a moment and look at that, please.

A: All right, sir.

Q: By the way, before I ask you about that, I want to ask you a couple of other questions about your denying Vic Feazells motion for *pro hac vice* to appear in your court. You denied that the same day he filed the motion, didn't you? Just bam, just like that, didn't you?

A: Could have been. I don't know.

Q: And isn't there some kind of ruling or case in the Fifth Circuit that basically says that a lawyer should be granted a hearing before his motion for *pro hac vice* is denied?

A: Not that I'm aware of sir.

Q: Judge, Pl's exhibit #140, tells us what that is please.

A: First page is a letter to Mr. Feazell from Ben Selman, Chairman of the District 86 Grievance Committee. The second page is a letter from me to Mr. Selman.

Q: Whets the date of that letter from you to Mr. Selman?

A: August 24, 1988.

Q: Judge, this has something to do with something that occurred---there is testimony about it with this letter – that has to do with a matter that occurred up in Sherman, Texas; does it not?

A: Yes sir. I believe that's right.

Q: And it didn't in any way, form or fashion deal with you directly, did it?

A: No sir.

Q: Would you tell the folks on the jury – just read your letter, if you would, please, who it's to and what you said.

A: To Mr. Ben Selman, Attorney At Law, Waco, Texas; reference Mr. Vic Feazell.

Dear Mr. Selman, The purpose of this letter is to make inquiry, state a complaint or express my serious concern, whichever is most appropriate. I do not have the knowledge of the workings of the Grievance Committee that I probably should since I am writing you in your capacity as Chairman. As you know, several months ago Mr. Feazell was, by consent decree, placed on a year's probation, the primary condition of which I assume was that he not again violate cannon of ethics. While he has since been quoted as having made some unfortunate statements the quotes from last Friday night's *Herald* exceeds any possible acceptable bounds.

Note: The letter went on for 3 pages. The point is, that the Honorable Judge Walter Smith still contends here during his sworn testimony that he doesn't have any hostility towards Vic Feazell.

Q: And Judge, had they agreed with you, Mr. Feazell would have lost his license to practice law most likely, wouldn't he have?

A: If his probation had been revoked, yes sir.

Q; And that's what you were hoping to see happen, wasn't it?

A: No sir. I was just calling this to their attention.

Q: Well Judge, they didn't agree with your assessment of what Mr. Feazell had done, did they?

A: No sir that's not correct.

Q: Well, did they in any way sanction Mr. Feazell?

A: Not that I am aware of.

Q: Judge, let me hand you a document that says that "at approximately 8:30 A.M. on the morning of

Tuesday, July 30, 1985, US Federal Judge Walter Smith approached Robert Zane (this was the head FBI agent working on Vic's criminal case). When did you first meet FBI agent Zane?

A: I don't recall.

Q: Would it have been before this occasion?

A: I don't know.

Q: And it goes on to say: "and Asst. US Attorney Jan Patterson (this is the one that was removed from Vic's criminal case because of her conduct), in Patterson's office in the Federal courthouse in Waco, Texas. Patterson and Zane were meeting in Patterson's office at that time with Investigator Ron Boyter, Texas Dept. of Public Safety. At this time Judge Walter Smith presented to Patterson and Zane an envelope containing two one—page letters, this envelope was addressed to Walter Smith with a return address of Carol Maynard, Waco, Texas, postmarked July 28, 1985. This letter was found to contain a one-page letter beginning, "Dear Council Member". Judge, do you have any idea how this document was made a part of Vic Feazell's investigative file with the FBI?

A: None. I have no memory *(here it comes again)* of this instance at all.

Q: Do you know why all the typewriters were taken from Mr. Feazells office?

A: No idea

Q: And this was a typewritten letter, right?

A: Yes

Q: Do you know, Judge, why also in Mr. Feazells investigative file from the FBI, why there's a document pertaining to an investigation of a drug ring?

A: No.

Judge, we pass the witness.

*Four years after this cross-examination of the
Honorable Judge Walter Smith, I was hired by
one of the individuals that escaped the fire in
Waco, Texas when the David Koresh
compound went up in flames. My client, David
Thibodaux (?) was one of seven that were
indicted. When I showed up to represent my
client, in Judge Walter Smith's courtroom,
much to my surprise, the US Attorneys office
dismissed the case against my client. The
word in the legal community in Waco was that
Judge Smith did not want me in his courtroom,
so he just had the charges dropped against my
client.*

CHAPTER 6

JUSTICE DELAYED IS JUSTICE DENIED

Judge's Behavior Thwarts Jury's Decision

"This'll kill us, Mr. Richardson," the man moaned over the telephone one morning in the spring of 1986. He and his two partners had just been told by Centennial Savings and Loan Bank in Greenville, Texas, that no additional funds would be advanced for their million-dollar apartment project which they had already started.

"We're dead in the water," the man went on. "Please, Gary, unless you help us, we're finished."

A mutual friend in Dallas had referred the caller and his associates to me. From the tremor in his voice, I could well imagine the anguish they were experiencing. It has always been my commitment to help those in need, especially people who had suffered either at the hands of the judicial system or the so-called "power structure." Often, the two forces were tightly intertwined.

I didn't know it at the time, but this occasion turned out to be one of those "unholy" alliances. I flew to Dallas to meet with my potential clients. Theirs was, once again, my type of case: the powerless versus the powerful.

###

During the mid-1980s, Centennial Savings and Loan Bank was a large and powerful financial presence in the small Hunt County community less that an hour's drive northeast of Dallas. After the completion and approval of the appropriate paperwork, the bank had made a commitment to lend more than a million dollars, in installments, to three of its most reputable customers – two prominent physicians, one of who lived in Dallas, and a local businessman - in order to construct an attractive apartment complex in a pleasant part of this small town, Greenville, Texas. They'd planned to call it "Gaslight Square Apartments," and it promised to be a unique asset to the area.

One of the partners, Dr. James E. Nicholson, a general medical practitioner in Greenville, was a likeable and well-respected family man and a community leader. Dr. Gary Hutchison, the other physician, was a renowned Dallas specialist. Their third participant was a successful local businessman and investor named Carl E. Eckman, who spearheaded the venture on behalf of the group.

Centennial advanced the initial funds as agreed, and construction had begun. For a few months, everything was precisely on schedule. The project was nearing the halfway point, and the partners were eager to complete their endeavor and begin generating revenues. However, one day, out of the blue, the bank notified them that because of a downturn in the local economy, no further monies would be available. They were not asked for any input. They were questioned about their abilities to perform. This unilateral and unexpected decision caught the partners totally off guard. Regardless of the favorable prospects of their particular project, even under the supposedly changed economic conditions, their dream died with one devastating phone call.

The stunned investors were in an untenable position. Half a loaf might be better than none in some situations, but in the building business, half an unfunded apartment is a disaster. Now, when one banking institution does as this one did, it's almost a certainty that another institution won't make the loan either. Not only were the men obligated to repay what they had already borrowed, they were denied the opportunity to complete the complex in order to generate the income needed to meet their indebtedness. Indeed, they were faced with the very real possibility that they would lose everything, including their personal solvency.

Greenville, Texas, though a smaller town, was in many ways like Waco. A tiny minority of its residents ran the place and dominated its institutions. Fortunately, most juries are aware of this unfortunate but customary connection, and the juries are frequently the only avenues an average citizen can rely on to level the playing field when a wrong has been committed.

In Judge Bosworth, the jurist assigned to hear the case, we thought we had a good and fair man. By reputation, he was someone who knew his role and didn't display favoritism toward any of the litigants. To our chagrin, we learned otherwise. Again, something I had seen too often in my career seemed to take over as we began displaying the appearance of winning against another powerful defendant.

The trial, which was held in Texas' 354th District Court, began in late May of 1986. It was a three-week, open-and-shut revelation of the facts. We had sued for $1,014,606 in actual damages -plus punitive - for seven breaches of contract and violations of the state's Deceptive Trade Practices Consumer Protection Act.

In my closing argument, I unashamedly told the jurors that my clients were clearly entitled to both sums for which they had suffered.

"Ladies and gentlemen, Centennial is your savings and loan bank. This is the institution you expect to be fair with you, just as you would be with them. Now that you've seen how they've treated my clients, two of whom are hard-working citizens of your community, plus a fine doctor from Dallas who wanted to do his part to make Greenville a better place in which to live, it's up to you to correct this injustice and send a message to the bank that good people are not to be treated this way. If you conclude that Centennial defaulted on its obligation, that what they did wasn't fair to my clients, and you want to get their attention to help prevent this abuse to others in the future - make an example out of them, in other words, by letting them know this type of conduct won't go unpunished – you can award punitive damages in addition to my clients' actual damages."

The jurors retired to deliberate shortly after noon on June 2, 1986. That evening, they returned and gave us $1,214,606 - $1,014,606 in actual expenses and lost profits and $200,000 in "discretionary" (punitive) damages. According to court clerk Ann Prince, this was the largest jury verdict award ever granted in Hunt County. Under Texas law, if the judgment was upheld on appeal, the damages could be trebled, making it a verdict in excess of $3Million.

Afterwards, in the hallway, one juror smiled, walked over to me, and said he'd wanted to do what was right and he believed he had. I thanked him for his courage.

"Mr. Richardson, I hope your people will now finish that apartment," the man added. He beamed. "We sure do need it. It'll make Greenville proud."

As in many situations when the defense loses, numerous motions can be filed to delay or attempt to subvert the jury's decision. For example, they can petition the judge to set aside the verdict (a "JNOV," the Latin abbreviation for "judgment notwithstanding the verdict"), claiming legal error in the record, and request a new trial. If the judge accedes, the result is as if the first trial never took place, and the defense gets another chance.

This is exactly the path that Centennial's lawyers chose. Even though it was a clean victory for us with the jury, I was genuinely concerned, as I always am, about what the defense might do to reverse its fortunes after losing in court. I was confident there had not been any legal error on the issues the judge had ruled on during the trial as the Judge had, throughout the trial given the bank practically everything they asked for, but I was worried that something else might be afoot, possibly a surprise issue we hadn't considered.

I had noticed throughout the trial that the judge often seemed pained whenever we made good point. I'm no psychologist, but I thought some sort of internal battle must be taking place in his mind: this dominant Greenville financial institution might actually lose its case, and the judge would have the power structure to answer to. Bosworth was not unlike many jurists in small communities: He was a political animal. Like other state judges, he had to stand for periodic reelection, and how the locals, especially the "big boys,' felt about his conduct on the bench could well be determined in his success at the polls. Centennial's loss might indeed spell his own.

There had been several incidents during the trial that revealed the judge's leanings against us. Just days before the courtroom proceedings began, the bank had hired a local Greenville lawyer to complement the two principle attorneys who were from a large Dallas firm. It obviously was no accident that this newly hired lawyer was the former partner of Judge Bosworth before Bosworth took the bench. Whenever we had to approach the bench, this local lawyer, who sat quietly and unobtrusively during the trial, was always the one who stepped forward to argue the defense's position directly to Bosworth. Virtually every time, the judge ruled in his favor. This obvious appearance of bias galled me. After several more adverse decisions, I could no longer restrain myself.

"Your honor, I'm getting real tired of your endless and obvious conclusions that this local attorney, your former partner, is the only one in the courtroom who knows anything about the legal process and what's appropriate."

Judge Bosworth glowered at me, but I continued. "You consistently agree with him when we approach the bench, no matter what he says. Good point or bad, he always gets a favorable ruling."

I turned and faced the local lawyer then looked over my shoulder at the other two Dallas lawyers, who were seated twenty feet away, waiting for their local hometown lawyer to prevail again.

"And I have tried more lawsuits than all three of these lawyers put together. I do know what I'm doing, but based on your rulings, it would appear that I don't know anything."

The local counsel responded while shaking his head. "Mr. Richardson," he protested, "Are you accusing this judge of giving you 'home-town' treatment?"

The man was a decent sort, but I was indignant. I put my hand on his shoulder. "Now that you mention it, that's exactly what I'm saying."

The lawyer lowered his head and returned to his seat.

Then, after another heated discussion, the judge ordered us to his chambers. From the way he scowled at me as we filed out of the courtroom, I knew he was furious and ready to chew on me and read me the right act, so to speak. He closed the door and stomped toward his chair. I have never been able to take a chewing very well. I don't give chewings, never have as that isn't my style, and I don't typically take them. I've always felt there were better ways to deal with a situation without demeaning someone. If someone works with or for me, I treat him or her with respect. If there's a problem, I sit down and attempt to resolve it. I make my points, but I never rant and rave. I don't try to take away anyone's dignity, and I don't allow that to be done to me. By the same token, I try to respect the position and feelings of any judge I face. However, if he's going to try to take advantage of my client, he's going to risk an all-out war.

I decided to do my best to disarm Bosworth before he could begin his tirade.

"By the way, judge," I opened as I walked into his chamber and, in my most neighborly tone of voice, asked, "Have you heard the one about the hunting dog named Lawyer?"

Judge Bosworth stopped before sitting down. He regarded me warily then replied with a curt, "No."

"Well, this is a great one, judge. I think you'll like it."

"Lawyer was the best hunting dog around. Whenever anyone wanted to do some serious hunting, they'd always ask for Lawyer. They knew if they hired Lawyer, he'd produce. Guaranteed. For example, of you wanted quail, he'd get quail. If you wanted rabbit, he'd get rabbit. I mean this dog was unbelievable. However, one day, some hunters took Lawyer with them, but he wouldn't do anything but just sit and howl. Finally, they got disgusted, and they took him back to his owner. 'What in the world has happened to Lawyer? All he has done today is sit and howl.'

"Lawyer's owner chuckled and replied, 'Well, I'll tell you. I guess he's ruined, I guess he won't ever get over it. Last week, some guys came out from Austin to go hunting. They had this big-time politician with them, and they insisted on having my best dog. Of course, that was Lawyer. Now, I normally didn't let Lawyer go out with hunters who didn't have a lot of experience, but they insisted. They wanted to impress the politician, so I let them take Lawyer. Lawyer started performing as he always had and this politician got so excited that he called him 'Judge' instead of Lawyer, and now all he wants to do is sit on his ass and howl."

I laughed at my own joke, but the judge didn't crack a smile. When he didn't chew me out, I was sure I'd made my point. By telling a joke, I'd kept the relationship on a relaxed level and showed him I wasn't intimidated, nor would I be. I was saying, "I know where your boundaries are, and I'm just as comfortable with you as you are with me. I'll do my job as a lawyer, and you'll do yours as a judge, but I will not be a cowering servant in this courtroom or any other." That which my father had planted in me was at work. He planted "No son of mine will ever be a coward," in me at age 15. And to please my father, whom I loved and admired so much, I determined to be that which he expected of me. That's how I became "fearless", just as a consultant who worked for me for years said when he was interviewed for a television show I was on, called *Oklahoma's Legal Top Gun*, and said "the thing that separates Gary from all the other lawyers I work for is that Gary is 'fearless'."

No lawyer can fairly represent his clients if he fears a judge. That's something I fervently believe. Otherwise, the system is out of balance, and justice, often; will not be served.

Minutes later, the judge overruled all of the defendant's motions. No hesitation, no explanation, just "denied". I was elated, as were my clients, and I felt that the battle could be finally over. Little did I know, I had forgotten the old expression that "there's often a slip between the cup and the lip."

###

A week or so afterwards, I prepared the judgment documents, and walked into Bosworth's office for his signature. The judge smiled and offered me a chair and took out his pen. He held it over the appropriate line on the paper as if prepared to sign, but then he paused and peered at me over the top of his bifocals.

"Has the other side seen this?"

I frowned. "Well, no, your honor, but they lost, we won, and this is consistent with the jury's verdict and your orders. Under the circumstances, I see no reason to have them review it."

The judge replaced the pen in its holder and clasped his hands over the paper.

"Maybe we oughta let them see it first."

The worries I had felt during the trial surfaced again, and I sighed.

"We can do it, but I can't. I mean, I don't understand why they need to see it. After all, it contains everything you ordered."

Bosworth leaned back in his chair and stared at the ceiling.

"Counselor, this is such a major step that I think they should have some time to think about it."

"Why, your honor?" I asked. "What could they object to? What's done is done."

As I spoke, I began to realize that the judge knew exactly what he was doing, he was obviously "insuring his re-election".

You see, my clients did not have near the political strength in Greenville as this large bank. I had a feeling that he intended to give the defense another chance. Looking back, the signs had been obvious all along. He was connected to the powerful. I was just one man representing three individuals.

"No, I'm going to give them more time," Bosworth concluded.

With nothing more to say, I stood up and left.

Sure enough, within hours, the defense was back. They made another motion to set aside the verdict and to grant a new trial, on the grounds that were later shown to be without merit. However, this launched a brand-new hearing, and the judge listened intently as Centennial's lawyers argued that my clients were not entitled to bring this case in the first place because they didn't meet the criteria of the state's consumer protection law. He had passed plenty of opportunities to raise this long before now, it there had been any basis to his allegation.

I couldn't believe my ears. Their argument was unfounded. If we didn't have the right to sue - a position which, if true, was indisputably crucial to the defense-why hadn't they raised this issue before the trial, or during the trial itself? It was obviously posturing by the defense, something pulled out of thin air at the last minute. Since they hadn't raised the matter earlier, it had been legally waived, and they were barred from raising it now. Bosworth shouldn't be giving it a second's consideration.

Indeed, the Texas deceptive trade act provided special protection for "consumers" whose net-worth didn't exceed a certain amount. In our case, the defense now argued, my clients had substantially greater net worth's, so they were not afforded the law's protection and therefore were barred from bringing an action under it, they argued.

"Your honor," I objected vociferously, "this is a factual matter which the other side has to prove in court. They didn't raise it during the trial, and this certainly isn't the forum to introduce it for the first time. The trial's *over*, the jury's made its decision, now the defense wants a 'special' trial in chambers."

I was furious. I started pacing to help dispel my anger.

"As a matter of fact, they don't have, and never did have, any evidence to substantiate their allegation. This is nothing but a ruse-desperate, last minute, and without merit."

Calmly, the judge glanced over at the lawyers for Centennial. There was no response, no papers were produced, and the men just sat in silence.

"Well," Bosworth finally responded, "I think they've made a very good point, so I'm going to have to give this some serious thought,"

I knew then what he was about to do, but he didn't want to say it in our presence. I was stunned that he was even considering this motion. The facts, the law, and the jury's decision were all in our favor, but Bosworth was improperly and unilaterally about to change the outcome to —. I could only shake my head in frustration. Across the room, Centennial's lawyers were grinning.

The judge rose to leave. "Good day, gentlemen," he offered.

Judge Bosworth, with one stroke of the pen, preserved his re-election and denied my clients justice. What we didn't know was that regardless, regardless of what the jury did or was going to do, we never had a chance to get justice. This was Black Robe Fever at its most malignant, its worst, and thank God that all judges are not more interested in re-election than in justice for the people.

After a moment, I grabbed my briefcase and headed for the motel. I couldn't believe what was happening. It was hours before I collected myself and began to plan our next step. Still, I couldn't believe that Judge Bosworth, by not requiring the defense prove that my clients didn't qualify as consumers under the law, had blatantly rejected a jury's decision.

Black Robe Fever was alive and well in Greenville, Texas, to the detriment of its many good citizens.

As soon as we had the legal right to do so, I appealed to the Court of Appeals in Dallas. I was certain that this flagrant example of judicial abuse would be quick work by the appellant judges. I felt even better about our prospects because I had learned a few days earlier that a similar case, "right on point," as we say, had been appealed to the Court of Appeals in Houston. There, the plaintiffs, who held the same position as ours, were victorious. I was certain that the Dallas court would consider the Houston case and decide in our favor. "Hope springs eternal," someone once said.

At the time we won our original verdict, Centennial Savings and Loan Bank had a net worth in excess of $6 million, so I was not concerned about collecting our judgment, plus accrued interest ...if, of course, we survived the appeals process, as we certainly expected. About the latter, I really had no concern. I was confident we would prevail. The law was solid and on our side on this issue.

It took two months for the Dallas court to act. I remember ripping open the certified letter the moment it arrived. I stared at the written opinion in disbelief.

Incredibly, Judge Bosworth's decision had been upheld. The ruling totally ignored what had already been resolved by another appellate court. The Houston case was precisely equivalent to ours, and the judges there had used clear and unambiguous language to explain why the plaintiffs in that case should prevail. On such simple issues of law, this disparity between two appellant courts was, and is, so rare as not to merit mention. It should have been open and shut. Why the Dallas court didn't agree with the Houston appellate court spoke volumes. But the question we couldn't answer was, "How can this be?"

I immediately appealed to the Texas Supreme Court. Only the highest authority could resolve the conflicting opinions by the two courts of appeal. As I mailed our petition, I hoped and prayed that the judges would see the vast similarities in the two decisions and rule in our favor. Somewhere deep inside, I knew they would.

One evening, a few days later, I received a call from Dr. Nicholson, my client, the physician living in Greenville.

"Gary you're not going to believe what happened last night." I sat up and listened as he related his story. "My wife and I went over to Dallas for dinner with our daughter who attends Southern Methodist University. We were seated at a table next to two couples that were engaged in a loud but friendly conversation that we couldn't help over hearing. I looked over and, to my surprise; I recognized Judge Bosworth and his wife. He and the other man were laughing while recounting their Navy days together and were apparently celebrating their anniversary of getting out of the service together. As they talked, I suddenly realized Bosworth's friend was the judge on the Court of Appeals in Dallas who had signed the order, which upheld Bosworth's decision against us. It was obvious they'd been close friends, like brothers, for a very long time."

I sat back in my chair. I now knew why the Dallas court had ruled against us.

It took two years, but we finally received the news we had hoped for. The Texas Supreme Court reversed Judge Bosworth and told him to enter a judgment in our favor. At first, we were ecstatic. But our celebration was short-lived. While our case was on appeal, Centennial Savings and Loan Bank had failed, and with it went our possibility of collecting our judgment. Time had definitely not been on our side.

Once Centennial went under, and the Resolution Trust Corporation took over, there was no one to pay my clients. The RTC came in and took over all of the bank's assets and wiped out all its debts. The result was an official, legal, rip-off of my clients, and this by a judge with Black Robe Fever. There was absolutely nothing we could do. The funding had stopped, and it wasn't about to resume. There was no insurance or anything else to soften the blow. My clients had been had by another "system" within our system of justice.

There's no law that judges can't have other judges as friends, but sometimes their friendships can delay — or deny — justice, as happened in our case. We won with the jury in Greenville, but, because of the Dallas judge's inappropriate and obvious ruling in favor of his friend, Judge Bosworth, irreplaceable time was lost.

In short, we won the battle but lost the war.

In the mid-to late- 1980s, Texas, as were many other states, was hurting from the depression of the petroleum industry. At the time of our verdict, the best information we had about the stability of Centennial was still positive. Maybe we were misled.

Someone later told me that Bosworth was aware of the bank's financial straits all along and that a delay might prevent my clients from collecting their judgment. The business and financial community probably did have such knowledge, but I honestly don't know if the judge did.

It's a fact that courts have a tendency to try and protect the local economy, including its institutions. But this isn't their job. This isn't justice. Their job is solely to mete out justice. Whether or not Judge Bosworth knew of Centennial's dire situation, the effect was the same. By thwarting the jury's decision, my clients were denied justice.

Judges are human, and as you can see, they can be influenced by the local establishment, the "power structure." Typically, reelection is always on their minds. They know which side their bread is buttered on, and who does the buttering. Upon reflection and it's only speculation on my part, I think that's what happened to us in this case. Bosworth's adverse ruling never should have been expected. Lawyers and their clients should be aware, however, that often what happens in the courtroom has its roots somewhere else. Black Robe Fever can have its foundation in many places, but regardless of the source, the result is destructive when the law is perverted, and the innocent suffer.

I end this Chapter by pointing out that I am just as quick to defend our Court system, as I am to point out Judges that corrupt it. To me, those few judges who corrupt the system aren't as great as the system itself. I think we have in America the best Court system in the world when it works and thankfully, I would say, that as a rule it does work and works the way it should. I never allow my clients to run down our court system. I always defend it and point out that it isn't the system that is bad, it's the few judges that had sand kicked in their faces when growing up that need to act tuff and/or the few judges that put their own futures before justice for all.

My philosophy is to never give up, to never quit believing in mankind or in our system of justice. I truly believe it is the best system in the world, and have on occasion debated the fairness of our system. Don't ever stop believing.

CHAPTER 7

ROUGH AS A COBB

A Wade in Deep Trouble

*It was my experience with
Judge Howell Cobb
that convinced me
to write this book.
He is amazing in his own way.*

Oklahoma's summers can be boringly predictable: oppressively hot and humid. July of 1988 was no exception. One sultry afternoon that month, I was in my Tulsa office reading depositions, listening to the radio, and wondering why the air conditioner couldn't keep up with my reasonable setting of 70 degrees. A disk jockey intoned that the temperature outside was just shy of the century mark." I winced and attempted to continue my work. The telephone rang.

"Mr. Richardson, my name is James W. Wade." The man's voice sounded measured. "I've just been wrongfully removed as sheriff of Orange County, Texas, and I'm in jail"

I jerked upright and pushed aside my paperwork.

"You're where?"

The man's voice continued in a matter-of-fact fashion. "I'm facing a ten-count federal indictment, including charges of conspiracy to manufacture a controlled substance, embezzlement of county funds, and obstructing justice." He became agitated. "Hell, my trial is only two weeks away!"

I attempted to calm him. I patted my desk as if to help tamp down his emotions. "OK, Sheriff Wade, now if you'll just tell me ..."

"For Christ's sake, Gary," he interrupted, "this judge is eating me alive. I don't stand a snowball's chance in hell. I need a new lawyer. I need you."

I tried again. "Sheriff Wade, please, just tell me exactly what's going on."

"The judge's running all over the guy who's representing me now. Every time we go to the courthouse, for motions or other appearances, we get killed. This judge is out of control."

"Who is the judge, sheriff?"

"Cobb." His voiced wavered. "U.S. District Judge Howell Cobb. He's out to get me, no matter what."

I attempted to maintain a low-key demeanor. "What makes you say that?"

"Damn it!" Wade exploded. "I'm a professional lawman, and I can see the handwriting on the wall. Cobb's going to crush me if I don't have a lawyer who'll stand up to him. I called you because of your reputation as someone who will aggressively represent his client, regardless of the circumstances."

At the time, I had no idea of the basis of Cobb's supposed bias against Wade, but that didn't matter. What I was most concerned with right then was for Wade to get a fair trial, which was guaranteed to him, at least in theory, under the United States Constitution.

"Please say you'll help me," he begged before I could tell him I was intrigued with his story, 'If nothing else, come down and hear my side of the story," he went on. "You don't have to take the case, but just having you here will give me some hope."

As soon as I could get a word in edgewise, I said I'd meet with him. If what he was saying was true, this was the type of case I wanted to handle. He was elated with my response. In his excitement, he almost hung up before I could ask him where he was being held.

"Lufkin," he answered. "East Texas, about a hundred and twenty miles northeast of Houston. Know where that is?"

"Sure do," I replied. "I used to live in Houston, went to law school there, and I've been in Lufkin many times. Matter of fact, my dad was a pastor there in a small Nazarene church."

After we spoke, I felt composed and thankful that Sheriff Wade had asked me for help. Little did I know that I was about to step into a massive snake pit. The Wade case was the worst misuse of power by a judge that I had ever encountered.***

###

The next day, I made the six-hour drive to Lufkin.

On the way, I remembered that the city had a population of about 30,000, and it was located deep in the heart of the beautiful pine woods country, surrounded by national forests. The huge Sam Rayburn Reservoir was nearby, and the area was one of the country's major lumber-producing regions.

A friend of mine had told me that James Wade was a little over six feet tall, and walked with his head held high. He was quite striking with flashing dark eyes and salt-and-pepper hair, which he kept trimmed in near-military style. His proud bearing came from a lifetime of dedication to public service - in the Air Force, as a Texas Highway Patrolman, as an ambulance attendant, and as a county sheriff.

But at our first face-to-face encounter in his jail cell, he seemed stooped, and, even as we shook hands, I noticed a sense of hopelessness reflected in his eyes. I realized that Wade was a man who'd lost faith in the future, any future. Standing, if that's the right word, before me was a distraught and depressed captive.

The two of us sat down on his bunk, and he began to reveal the details of his life, which had led to his imprisonment. Just after he started, he laughed. "Talk about a screwed up world. I went in as sheriff to clean up a county, and this is what I get."

I was glad to see evidence that not all of his self-esteem was gone. It also told me that I might be able to expect the truth from him. Humor, especially the self-deprecating variety, is often a sign that the individual is more genuine than not. Underneath whatever facade to the contrary, I was relieved to see that he was well balanced psychologically, so it seemed.

As he continued his story, I knew I would take the case. When he finished, some three hours later, I told him I was inclined to believe that what he had said was true and that it surely looked like he's been steamrolled by forces I didn't yet understand. I wasn't certain I could help him, but I wanted to try. He gave me a tight bear hug. There were tears in his eyes.

The story behind how Sheriff James Wade landed in jail is as bizarre as the trial that followed. To me, it's a shameful saga and a bitter indictment of a justice system that can be perverted by people out of control. It was as Lord Acton wrote, "Power tends to corrupt, and absolute power corrupts absolutely."[2]

Orange County, Texas, an hour's drive east of Houston on Interstate 10, had been a hotbed of drug trafficking for years, made easier because the region is a tangle of waterways and a short distance from New Orleans, and by air, from Mexico, Central and South America.

This pirate's paradise was a nest of little towns perched on or near many bodies of water in a niche of far southeast Texas. Orange County's east boundary is the Sabine River, the state line with Louisiana. The west county line is the Neches River; and Hardin, Jasper, and Newton counties form the northern perimeter. The Neches and Sabine rivers flow into a basin forming Sabine Lake, the county's southern border, before it empties into the Gulf of Mexico through a narrow channel called Sabine Pass. Through all of this the Intracoastal Waterway cuts along the west and north shores of Sabine Lake en route from Mexico to Louisiana and the East Coast.

It was into this geographic jumble and politically "active" territory that James Wade ventured to tackle the drug problem. He ran for sheriff in 1984, won, and took office on January 1, 1985.

Wade quickly began to get results. Year-end statistics for 1987 showed that overall crime was down four percent in the county-not a precipitous drop, but nonetheless progress in a jurisdiction not necessarily celebrated for its peaceful ways. Under his leadership, Wade and the 84-member Orange County Sheriff's Department were twice featured on the cover of the Texas Narcotics Officer's Association magazine for their fight against illegal drugs. They were even commended by the governor for being "Number one in Texas for drug-related arrest."

Unfortunately for Wade, however, his efforts were succeeding too well for the comfort of a certain segment of the

---

[2] Lord Acton wrote this in a letter to Bishop Mandell Creighton, 1887.

local population, and what he got for his good intentions and hard work was more trouble than he could have ever imagined.

In October of 1987, Donnie James Flowers, one of Wade's drug informants, was arrested while attempting to set up a drug lab in nearby Hardin County. Wade was completely unaware of Flower's illicit activities. Nonetheless, shortly after the arrest, rumors began flying that Wade himself was under investigation for involvement in illegal drug activities.

The FBI announced in late January, 1988, that the sheriff was indeed the subject of an investigation "after receiving information from an informant that Wade allegedly had been involved in the manufacture and sale of methamphetamine."

The local media had a field day. There was a myriad of stories about the investigation, each one more lurid and damning. With his reelection only six weeks away, Wade no longer suspected that he was being set up. He was certain of it.

During his campaign effort two months later, Wade placed newspaper ads in the Orange, Texas, newspaper in which he proclaimed his innocence and attempted to quell the rumors, including an egregious one that he was under investigation by the FBI for murder. In one of his rambling pleas, he argued:

"It is my feeling that many of the citizens and voters of Orange County have been confused, and mislead (sic), by the allegation and accusations that have been made against me. I have been attacked from every angle, with practically every type of rumor, accusation, and innuendo possible. However, those who have personally contacted me with any of the above-mentioned, I have been able, with facts and the truth, to prove the statements being spread are untrue. "
... I have broken NO laws of Orange County, The State of Texas, or The United State of America.

"There is an evil working in this county that does not want the average citizen to have a say in Orange County government. I do not agree with those who want to have total control of Orange County and for this reason they want me out of their way and will go to any extreme, or any amount of money, to GET ME OUT OF THE WAY. (Wade's emphasis)

"If there were facts and proof to support any of the allegations being lodged against me, don't you think I would have been indicted and/or arrested?

"If all of this 'so-called' information against me was available in October, 1987, WHY did they wait until six weeks prior to the election to hit the newspapers and television.

"There is NO murder investigation being conducted by the FBI involving me. Now if the Orange County D .A. 's office and the Orange Police Department felt that murder took place back in September of 1987, WHY did they wait until five weeks prior to the election to initiate an investigation and then insinuate that I was involved."

The answer is quite clear. This was a very devious plot, cleverly planned and orchestrated to destroy James Wade, politically, and to bring drug enforcement in Orange County to its knees. At this time, I do not feel that the FBI is a part of this plot, but that they are merely doing their job.

"I have been advised, by very reliable resources, that if they are not successful in their goals, the Drug Lords would have killed me. They are fooling the FBI with this investigation. "According to the U.S. Attorney, Bob Wortham, the Gulf Coast, which includes Orange County, has been designated as the area by drug smugglers from South America. Those in Orange County who wish to receive LARGE FINANCIAL GAINS from these operations do not want an honest sheriff in the way. What it amounts to is "WADE IS IN THE WAY." They want me out at any cost.

"I have discussed the matter with my family and their decision, as well as mine, is that I will stand up and WALK TALL for all the children of Orange County, as well as my own."

Wade faced three opponents in the Democratic primary on March 8, 1988. He survived round one, but was defeated in a run-off on April 2. Rumors and negative media stories had destroyed his credibility.

Weeks later, he was hit with a ten-count indictment by a Federal grand jury. The charges included conspiracy to make and sell drugs, embezzlement from Orange County's special drug-buy program, and obstruction of justice. On July 11, 1988, without the benefit of a trial or other legal proceeding, he was suspended from office by a state district judge.

During my jailhouse interview with Wade, I learned that he had brought in more law enforcement and Federal authorities to work at cleaning up the drug problem than any other lawman in the history of Orange County. The irony was that he ended up being indicted himself.

It made no sense whatsoever that Wade would summon all of those Federal and drug enforcement officials to uncover illegal drug activities if he were personally involved in the drug business. But a lot of powerful people, including law enforcement officers, are involved in the drug business, and some are even accepted as reputable members of their communities. Yet, the whole legal system was in tandem against a man who had fought to stop the pervasive trafficking of illegal substances. They refused to look at it from the standpoint of "maybe this guy is being setup."

In my opinion, James Wade was set up, and those who were behind this travesty did a heck of a job. If you buy the theory that he was set up, then you can see how it was done, and most everything about the case makes sense. Without that premise, nothing about the case makes sense. It often depends on how you look at a situation.

As an illustration, suppose a man loses his job, and he's flat broke. His wife tells him, "Honey, we're out of food. The kids haven't eaten in two days." He shrugs and leaves. An hour or so, he's back, with a loaf of bread, a gallon of milk, and a pound of bologna. His excited wife greets him at the door. "This is wonderful. How'd you get it?" The husband explains that he stole the food from a local grocery store, but he asks her to keep track of the items because as soon as he gets a job, he's going back to the store to pay for everything. Today, he's her hero. A year later, they're in divorce court. Same facts, but now he's judged a crook by the very same person who'd considered him her idol earlier.

My point is that one can take the same facts and reach different conclusions. The facts, which were used against Wade, could just as easily have made him a hero. The government called him a drug dealer, yet the same facts could have shown him as a heroic crusader against drugs in Orange County.

The way Sheriff Wade was railroaded was methodical and well planned. At times, it was also ludicrous. Wade was jailed before his trial, not on the charges for which he later was indicted, but, believe it or not, for selling his drug dog, Matthew.

It was during my second or third meeting with the sheriff that I met Frank Miller, an investigator who lived in Vidor, Texas.

"Frank knows everything about the case," Wade explained. "He's not only been very supportive but also very helpful in gathering evidence for the trial."

Miller told me the story of "the Matthew incident."

"All the conspiracy and drugs and everything else fell to the wayside, and they put Wade in jail for selling a dog," Miler said with gall in his voice. "There were several hearings about the matter, and Wade eventually won because it was proved the dog was a personal gift to him." Miller sneered. "As a matter of fact, the judge on that hearing, U.S. Magistrate Earl Hines, called in the prosecution. I believe he called them, 'overzealous prosecutors. '

"What happened was, while Wade was sheriff, he was given this pooch named Matthew. The donors testified that the dog was a personal gift, not one to the Orange County Sheriff's Department. They even presented documents they had asked Wade to sign, recognizing that Matthew was a personal gift. If and when Wade left Orange County, he could take the dog with him. They insisted on the paperwork because Orange County is so corrupt that someone might try to make something of this gift."

Miller continued. "It was after Wade was arrested for selling his dog that the U.S. government stepped in and picked up the prosecution. They were looking for an excuse to put the sheriff behind bars, and when they saw that the charges over Matthew were going to fall through, they cut deals with alleged drug dealers Nyle Henry 'Hank' Baker and Donnie Flowers in order to make sure Wade didn't get out of jail."

Hank Baker was a known felon who had been arrested in December, 1985, and convicted of involvement in a methamphetamine lab. As a result of what Flowers told government officials after his arrest in October, 1987, the FBI tied

Baker to Wade and indicted the two of them on one count of conspiracy to make and sell drugs.

Flowers had told the FBI two things: that Wade arranged for Baker's parole to be transferred to Orange County in 1987, after Baker' release from prison, and that Baker organized the alleged drug operation run by Wade.

Baker's attorney, Thomas Roebuck, asked that his client's trial be severed from Wade's because Baker was charged in connection with only one count of the 10-count indictment against Wade. Judge Cobb granted the motion.

"All we had to do was get Baker on the stand." Miller sighed in frustration. "That's what we planned. All Nyle Baker had to do was tell the truth. Get up on the stand and say, "You guys are nuts. I've never done anything with Wade.'

"But when Baker's case was separated from Wade's, it was reported that the government stepped in and said, 'Nyle, you're going to jail unless you cooperate. What we want you to do is cooperate with us by not cooperating with anyone else. If you testify for us, against Wade, we won't press charges against you. If you testify for Wade, we're going to send you to jail.'

"The government put all of this in writing, but Judge Cobb sealed it so that nobody could look at it."

I had certainly been warned about U.S. District Judge Howell Cobb, but nothing quite prepared me for the unique brand of injustice he seemed to relish dishing out. James Wade's trial hadn't even started, yet I already knew we were up against a stacked deck. I just didn't know how crooked the hand being dealt really was.

Within minutes of the beginning of the pretrial hearing, it was obvious that Judge Cobb despised Wade. Cobb also quickly directed his ire at me. This was definitely going to be an experience I'd never forget.

Earlier, I'd learned that when Wade was arraigned prior to hiring me, he was released on bond under one condition: that he not make any contact with the Orange County Sheriff's Department, even though he was still sheriff! But the "powers-that-be" weren't content with this restriction. They wanted him jailed. After Wade sold his "controversial" dog, a deputy sheriff drove out to the Wades' homes to deliver a check. Without any reason to be suspicious, Neva, the sheriff's wife, went out to the car to get the check. The next morning, the U.S. Attorney's office filed a motion alleging that her action violated the court's requirement that Wade have no contact with the sheriff's office. Incredibly, there were several hearings over this silly matter, but, also as incredibly, Judge Cobb revoked Wade's bond and sent him to jail.

On July 14, 1988, Cobb announced that he was moving the trial to Sherman, Texas, some 350 miles to the north, because of the excessive publicity about the case in Orange. Wade's then-attorneys, John Hannah of Tyler, a former U.S. Attorney, and Roger Moss of Lufkin requested the change of venue to Grayson County. Trial date was set for August 15.

Jeff Kearney, my co-counsel, and I took over the case at the end of July. We immediately filed a motion for continuance of the trial. If the August date was not changed, we'd have only two weeks to prepare. Given the many detailed circumstances, it looked to be an impossible task, yet we were confident based on our prior experiences that the motion for more time to prepare would be granted. The government, after all, had been preparing for seven months for the fiasco that was about to ensue.

It was not granted. Judge Cobb ruled against our motion and let the trial date stand — Black Robe Fever at its hottest, most flagrant pitch. Forget justice in this courtroom.

Based on what I had seen and had been told about Cobb's attitude by Wade, by his former attorneys, by several other attorneys, and by Frank Miller, I had a clue what it would be like to lock horns with this judge. It was something I wasn't looking forward to, but nonetheless, something I fully expected.

Looks, as they say, can be deceiving. Judge Howell Cobb was living proof. His exterior was the epitome of a kind, grandfatherly type. He stood about five feet nine inches tall, sported silver-streaked hair and a distinguished looking moustache, and he was always well dressed. "Dapper" is perhaps a good word to describe him. I'm sure many women considered him handsome.

Cobb descended from a line of judges going back to his great-grandfather, Howell Cobb, a Civil War general, after whom he was named. His great-grandfather was Secretary of the Treasury from 1857 to 1860 under President James Buchanan. His ancestor was reported to have had a penchant for serious partying at taxpayers' expense.

In a book entitled, *The President's House*, author William Seal wrote that the treasury secretary got into trouble for throwing a large drinking rendezvous for one of his constituents on a riverboat. When President Buchanan learned of the illegal funding of the shindig, he made Cobb pay the money back to the government. A passage in the book reads, "For in society, the Howell Cobbs were a law unto themselves." It seems that the great-grandson was doing his best to keep the family tradition alive.

Frank Miller advised me it was well known in Southeastern Texas that Judge Cobb had a drinking problem and, on many occasions, would take the bench after a long night with the bottle. "I've learned first-hand it's true," Miller assured me.

Miller also told me it was the general opinion in the Beaumont area that Cobb "had something to do with the death of his first wife" who was in perfect health but who died mysteriously at the age of 39 from a supposed fall in the bathtub."

"There was no investigation of her death,: Miller said. "The justice of the peace who handled the case is deceased, and all of the records are either sealed or destroyed. The opinion here is that Howell Cobb killed her." Miller then warned me. "Judge Cobb is well connected in the small, select system of justice within our judicial system. It's sad, but, nonetheless, that system is still in place," he sighed.

###

"Dapper" or not, once we started trial on August 16, 1988, Judge Cobb was congenial and accommodating to the government attorneys, but he wasn't to Jeff Kearney and me. Outside the courtroom, he was polite to us, but he seemed to change colors like a chameleon once he put the black robe on and strode into the courtroom. It was that conduct which mattered to me and really bothered me.

On the third day of the trial, attending journalists got a taste of the bitter medicine that Cobb later dispensed in even larger doses to Wade, Kearney, and me. While I was cross-examining Hardin County sheriff, H.R. "Mike" Holzapfel, a major witness for the prosecution, the judge abruptly closed the courtroom to the public and the media.

Holzapfel had just commented that he couldn't answer my question because of a pending case in state court.

The media was outraged and filed letters of protest with Cobb as well as with two members of the Federal judiciary: William Wayne Justice, chief judge of Texas' Eastern Judicial District and Charles Clark, the chief judge of the Fifth Circuit Court of Appeals. The wire services were white-hot with the story of Cobb's "patently offensive- and-contrary-to-precedent" behavior. The *Houston Post's* Ira Perry, who was also regional director of the Society of Professional Journalists, demanded that a transcript of Holzapfel's testimony to the jury be made available at once. The judge's action, he said, was in violation of U.S. Supreme Court's decisions regarding the conduct of Federal criminal trials, which must remain open unless there has been a prior hearing to determine that certain testimony may be given in secret.

When Judge Cobb was informed of the complaints being filed, he reportedly welcomed them. "Have at it, boys," he was heard to say. After all, this man in the black robe felt he owned the courtroom. That is one of the signs of a Judge that has Black Robe Fever and typically is a bully, they have come to think it is "their" courtroom and forget it belongs to the people and that the people pay for it, pay their income, etc, and they are there as a Judge, to do what judges are suppose to do, make rulings much like a referee in a ballgame.

In an August editorial in *The Orange Leader*, which was written a few days after Judge Cobb's arbitrary decision, the newspaper declared, "A Federal judge can't control the weather but otherwise rates as pretty close to godlike in running his courtroom." The editorial writer stated that Cobb's behavior was nothing unexpected. The judge regarded press coverage as a nuisance and the public's right to know hardly worthwhile. He'd imposed an all-encompassing gag order on February 3, and anyone with any knowledge of the case was forbidden to talk. "But actually little recourse exists against someone in Cobb's position," the editorial concluded. "A Federal judge is accountable only to the U.S. Senate, which may remove a judge through impeachment. That occurs only rarely and for outright illegalities - not matters as trivial as highhandedly closing the trial of Orange County's sheriff to the public. So Cobb is safe and sitting pretty. Unfortunately, the same cannot be said for the public's interest."

Obviously, our problems had begun even before we started offering our defense. It kept getting worse. I recall a major confrontation in the middle of the second week of trial.

Judge Cobb mumbled a lot. He drank excessively and was on medication, even during the trial, or so I was told. The combination of the two obviously contributed to his mental confusion, and, on occasion, everyone in the courtroom had difficulty hearing and understanding him.

On this particular day, I was cross-examining drug dealer Donnie Flowers, the key witness for the prosecution, when Cobb began to mumble something. Then he stopped, and there was a long pause. I thought he was finished, so I went back to cross-examining Flowers.

Cobb started mumbling again. "You're interrupting me, Mr. Richardson!'

"What, your honor?"

There had already been tension between the judge and me before now. This time, he decided to embarrass me in front of the jury.

"Don't interrupt me, counselor," he boomed. "You never interrupt a Federal judge!"

I stared at him, bewildered.

"Watch my lips," he snarled belligerently. "If my lips are moving and sound is coming out, then I'm talking."

He added a few other sarcastic remarks before allowing me to continue.

At the break, I told his clerk that I wanted to make a record. She acknowledged my request just as her telephone rang. She picked up the handset, whispered a few sentences, nodded, and then turned in my direction.

"Sir, the judge wants to see you in his chambers."

I shook my head and departed.

"What do you want to make a record about?" Cobb demanded in his deep, gruff voice.

"You'll find out when I make it," I informed him politely. "I want you to get your court reporter."

Cobb stared at me for what seemed like a full minute. He punched his intercom and asked for the court reporter and the other lawyers to come to his chambers. They arrived shortly thereafter. The court reporter took a seat at the edge of the judge's desk. When the man nodded he was ready, I made my record.

"Judge, I want you know that I have broad shoulders, and I can damn sure take an ass-chewing, but there's a proper place and time for everything. And the proper place and time for you to chew my ass is not in front of a jury when all I'm trying to do is my very best to see that a man gets his constitutional right to a fair trial."

"Furthermore, the reason you chewed me out is because you said I interrupted you, and, yes, I did, but so has every other lawyer in the courtroom, and there happens to be a very good reason for that. About half the time when you're sitting up there on the bench, you're mumbling, and we don't really hear you. The other half, you stop so long between sentences that we think you're through talking, so we start talking, and then you start talking again. To you, that's tantamount to an interruption. That's just what happened a few minutes ago in the courtroom."

"Your honor, if you'll quit mumbling on the bench and quit stopping so long between sentences, I'll do my best not to interrupt you in the future." The judge made a face. My statement obviously didn't mollify him. "And I have something else to say, sir." I took a step closer to where he was sitting. "Please never embarrass me in front of the jury again. The record will show that I kept my composure and conducted myself in the manner in which I thought our profession called for in the courtroom. I expect the same conduct and consideration from the bench. What just happened in there contributed nothing to the positive image of our profession."

Judge Cobb drew in a long breath and sighed as he exhaled. "Mr. Richardson, you're right. I do mumble a lot on the bench, and I do stop a bit long between sentences. I'll do my best to speak up where you all can hear me, and I'll try not to give the impression that I'm through talking when I'm not."

All of us in his chambers were stunned by Judge Cobb's response, but it further reminded me and confirmed what my dad had so often said — that "abusive" people are cowards. Judge Cobb certainly fit the bill. He was both. A number of lawyers called me and congratulated me for not letting him run over me, as he had done to lawyers so many times over the years.

He motioned for us to leave his chambers and return to the courtroom, which we did. But from that point on, I kept a ledger, writing down everything Judge Cobb did during the rest of the trial, anything that I thought was prejudiced against my client, James Wade — much of which would never be reflected on the record because it wasn't verbal. Things like facial expressions. For example, he would roll his eyes or swivel his chair if he thought my co-counsel Jeff Kearney or I made a point with a witness against the government's case. By such conduct, he'd let the jury know he didn't think it was a good point, that what we had just scored was insignificant.

Sometimes he even made a comment such as, "So what is that supposed to mean?"

All during the trial, Cobb's facial expressions, mannerisms, and tone of voice were derogatory toward my co-counsel and me. And if we made an objection, regardless of its merits, Cobb would often give us a disgusted look.

"I had never seen a judge treat attorneys the way Cobb treated Gary and Jeff," Frank Miller remarked. "Gary, in particular, was treated worse than a stepchild. The military refers to it as 'Delta Sierra.' Furthermore," Miller emphasized, "Judge Cobb was drunk much of the time during Wade's trial."

Sometimes the prejudicial nature of the trial was not even close to being subtle. Miller recalled that one of the most flagrant displays of prejudice against Wade was by the U.S. Marshal in charge of the jury.

"While the trial was underway, the marshal played with a piece of rope. Sitting in full view of the jury and the court, he constructed a hangman's noose, but after all, he was the marshal," Miller said in disbelief.

Judge Cobb didn't seem to notice.

Another example of the bias against Wade was visual. Miller said, "For hearings and during the whole trial, he was paraded into the courtroom in shackles. Our client was handcuffed with his hands chained to his wrist, and his feet manacled. They treated him like a serial killer, a dangerous criminal, and they kept him in a jail cell so small he could barely move."

Wade wasn't the only target. Attempts were also made to implicate Miller of wrongdoing. While the trial was underway, Miller's personal airplane was tampered with by government officials, a Federal offense, and documents were stolen.

"The Feds broke into my airplane on two occasions during the trial and took papers," Miller fumed. "I reported it as soon as I learned about it. You see, I was using the airplane to fly around in my investigation for Wade's case, and the Feds were trying everything they could to make anybody who had anything to do with Wade, even then, a criminal.

Miller continued, "I had been unable to figure out who exactly, was breaking into my personal airplane until, during the course of one of the hearings, Paul Naman with the U.S. Attorney's office stood up and waved my flight log and all the other materials that had been removed from my plane. We brought this to Judge Cobb's attention, but nothing ever came of it."

"Tampering with an aircraft is an extremely dangerous thing to do," Miller emphasized, still incensed. "After the first break-in, we discovered that the Feds had inspected our wing tanks, evidently to make sure we only had fuel and weren't hauling whatever they thought we were hauling." He laughed. "Well, they left the caps off. Now, if you're not familiar with an airplane, the caps are on top of the wings. If you fly with the caps off, the air passing over the wings will siphon the fuel out as you fly, or if it rains, you have water in the fuel! Believe me, leaving the caps off isn't something that a competent pilot does. I mean, it's a serious error. Only an idiot would do it!" Miller stewed.

Miller sat in silence for a moment of reflection. Then, he shook his head.

"Another time the Feds broke in, they either bumped up against our compass and broke it accidentally or did it on purpose. Either way, they also altered the readings on one of our gauges. Fortunately," he continued, "we discovered what had happened both times during our preflight checks. But I finally had to put a guard on my plane around the clock, just to keep anyone from jacking with it."

"I wrote a letter to the President and the U.S. Attorney General, and it's actually been assigned a case number."

"The FBI is supposed to investigate anything having to do with tampering with aircraft," Miller said sarcastically, "when it's the FBI doing the tampering, you're sure as hell not going to have an investigation. The FBI has covered it all up. This whole trial is a cover-up."

Judge Cobb did many things throughout the trial to undermine my ability to defend Wade. And he did absolutely nothing like this to the government attorneys. A prime example was when I was cross-examining drug dealer Donnie Flowers, the prosecution's star witness. This was after the "mumbling" incident with Cobb and my questioning was going well. Frank Miller enjoyed telling what happened next.

"Suddenly, during Gary's line of questioning, Judge Cobb stood up in his bench, which a judge just never does."

"Objection!" he roared.

Miller laughed at the recollection. "The courtroom went into an absolute stall. Even the prosecutors sat there with their mouths open. Cobb mumbled several sentences that nobody could understand. Then he evidently decided that he wanted the prosecution to object and told them to do so. Finally, Paul Naman, the assistant U.S. Attorney, reluctantly stood and said, 'Your Honor, we'll object.'"

"Judge Cobb then mumbled something else, overruled his own objection, and sat back down. I was flabbergasted," Miller said, "as was the rest of the court."

That incident was completely removed from the trial transcript. The court reporter, Benny L. Walker, did what many court reporters do - he protected his boss, the judge. Walker simply deleted sections of the trial and addenda to the records made in the judge's chambers that he felt would show Judge Cobb in a bad light.

Cobb was not without his assets, however. He was quite a master at getting the jury's confidence - in him. A tactic some judges use to placate and ingratiate the jurors is to spend time talking to them. Then, frequently, he can get by with almost anything. Not all judges use this tactic, but those who do obviously intend to endear themselves to the jury, which, usually, makes the judge more powerful. Well, Judge Cobb was good at that. If a jury doesn't like the judge, or if the judge is remote, or stays in a more professional mode and doesn't try to seduce the jury, then he or she typically has less influence over the jury. But it was pretty obvious to me that Cobb worked hard at getting the jury to like him.

One morning during the trial, Judge Cobb called all the attorneys into his chambers. Cobb wanted to know if any of us had anything we wanted to say to him or if there was anything we wanted to bring up. I didn't have any idea what he was talking about, and none of the other lawyers seemed to either. I did note that the judge seemed befuddled as he wandered around the room.

We didn't put it all together until two or three days later. What we learned that he was concerned about had been kept hush-hush, but it finally hit the newspapers: Judge Cobb had been arrested for driving while intoxicated during the trial. I checked my trial calendar notes and realized that Cobb's arrest had taken place in the early hours of the morning he called us unexpectedly in to see if there was anything we wanted to bring up. Obviously he was concerned. He probably thought we knew about his arrest, but we didn't. We found out later by reading the newspaper account.

Judge Cobb had been stopped and arrested by a state trooper for speeding and suspicion of drunk driving in Denison, Texas, on August 31. According to Sergeant Charles Carey of the Department of Public Safety, Cobb was accused of driving 70 mph in a 55-mph zone. Trooper Y.Q. Tillery filed the speeding charge against Cobb and presented a driving-while-intoxicated case to Grayson County Attorney, Steve Davidchik, who said the trooper's report had been submitted but that no charges would be filed until after the James Wade trial ends.

At the time, Cobb declined to comment to the media on his arrest.

Carey said that Cobb was taken to the Grayson County Jail, where he refused to take a breath analysis test. According to newspaper reports, Sheriff L. E. "Jack" Driscoll said he agreed to allow the judge to be booked after the trial, adding that such considerations are not uncommon in "extenuating circumstances."

A week after the trial was over, the *Fort Worth Star-Telegram* confirmed the report that Cobb had refused a routine sobriety test.

The same day the Ft. Worth paper perfunctorily reported the incident, the *Sherman Democrat*, in an editorial entitled, "Judge Knows How to Handle DWI Arrest," observed, "There's something unsettling about a Federal judge - arrested for drunk driving and speeding - managing to avoid normal booking procedures and disclosure of his offense for ten days. It happened with the cooperation of law enforcement officials in Sherman who say he received no preferential treatment.

The story continued, "If it hadn't been for leaks to the news media, Judge Howell Cobb's arrest probably would still be a secret.

"Endangering lives on a public highway is a serious offense, but compromising the conduct of a major trial and allowing human frailty to compound the public's distrust in their officials are even more troubling.

"Judge Cobb is presiding over the protracted corruption trial here of suspended Orange County Sheriff James Wade. Through his attorney, Judge Cobb managed to slip out of jail without leaving his mug shot, fingerprints or evidence he'd ever been there. He promised to return and face his accusers when the trial concluded.

"Cobb denies that he asked for any favor, nor, he says, was given any. That's really beside the point. The Cobb case brings into clear focus Grayson County's accepted practice for handling first-time DWI suspects. Is the existing policy fair, or should a stricter policy be enforced ...

"Judge Cobb will get his day in court, but his handling of this personal crisis reflects badly on him and on his public trust."

The fact that this information came to light without any repercussions to Federal Judge Howell Cobb is even more disturbing.

###

When Judge Cobb called us into his chambers that morning, he should have informed us that he'd been out drinking all night, to the point that he was arrested for DWI, so the attorneys involved in the trial could decide whether or not he was fit to conduct trial that day.

Similarly, if a lawyer is out drinking during the night to the extent that he becomes intoxicated, such as Cobb obviously was, resulting in his being arrested, that lawyer owes a duty to his client to say, "Hey, I may not be operating to my full capacity today." If he doesn't do that, then he has some liability.

But this tip of the Cobb iceberg, though treacherous, left far more of the iceberg below the surface — frighteningly cold — unobserved by most.

Two or three weeks after the mumbling episode when I made the first record, Judge Cobb chewed out my co-counsel in front of the jury. At the break, I told Judge Cobb's bailiff that I wanted to make another record. On this occasion, I pointed out in detail all the additional things he was doing in the courtroom, which I thought were making it impossible for James Wade to get a fair trial. I emphasized that when certain witnesses testified, the judge rolled his eyes as if to say, "Yeah, give me a break." It was apparent to me that he was trying to communicate to the jury.

After the trial, that record was never made a part of the appeal filed on Wade's behalf. It, too, had been deleted from the trial transcript, but more on that later.

When the trial was finally over, and the jury was deliberating, Judge Cobb came into the courtroom where the lawyers had gathered to await the jury's return, and asked me to join him in his chambers, which I did.

"Richardson," he started as soon as I stepped inside his office, "it looks like you may walk this man out of the courtroom."

"Well, judge," I responded, "that's going to be pretty tough to do, but maybe we have a fifty-fifty shot at it."

"To tell you the truth," Cobb remarked, "1 hope you don't win."

"That's been fairly obvious from the beginning," I told him, "but now that the trial's over, maybe you'll tell me why you feel the way you do."

"I'll tell you after the jury comes back," he said.

We continued talking then, without any encouragement from me, Cobb volunteered, "Well, I'll go ahead and tell you now why I said that. It doesn't have anything to do with the case, but Benny Walker, my court reporter, is in financial straits. He has a loan due at the bank and could use the money."

What he meant was that if Wade was convicted, an appellate record would have to be ordered, and his court reporter would receive a handsome fee for it, some $42,500, as it turned out.

When Cobb made that statement, I stood up and said, "Judge, I think it's best that I leave your chambers."

He held up his hand. "Before you go, I'd like to ask you a favor."

"Oh, and what's that?"

"I'm asking that you don't tell anyone what I just said."

I thought I'd heard everything, but this was the pinnacle. I shook my head in disgust.

"Judge, I'm sorry, but the oath of office I took doesn't allow me to conspire with you against the best interests of my client. I will be filing a motion to have you removed from this case," I said, "and I will put everything you just said in the motion."

With that, I turned and walked out of his chambers.

In September of 1988, after a six-week trial, a jury of nine men and three women convicted James Wade of nine counts of conspiracy to make and sell drugs, distribution of controlled substances, and obstruction of justice. He faced up to one hundred and fifteen years in prison and fines of more than $4 million.

Without question, Judge Cobb should have recused himself from the Wade trial because of his blatant bias against the former sheriff. We filed a motion asking that Judge Cobb be removed from further proceedings in the case. It contained a recitation of the examples of bias we had observed, including the inappropriate conversation he had with me in chambers while were waiting for the jury to return.

One woman that we learned through an investigator Cobb had been seeing "socially," told an investigator that the judge had earlier whispered to her he hoped he'd get assigned the Wade case, because he was going "to help hang him." We also asked for

Wade to be released pending sentencing and a new trial or acquittal.

I went to Beaumont for the hearing.

I was the first witness to testify at this hearing. I took the stand voluntarily and testified, after being sworn in, about the conversation I had with Judge Cobb in his chambers, when he told me that he hoped we didn't walk Sheriff Wade out of the courtroom and why he felt that way. After I testified, and before any other witnesses were called to testify, Judge Cobb stopped the proceedings and told the lawyers to come to his chambers.

"What else do you have, Richardson?"

"Beg your pardon?"

"Other than this ...lady?" he sputtered.

I took a deep breath. "You'll find out when we get back in the courtroom, Your Honor."

Judge Cobb then stood, told his reporter that this would be off the record, and said to my co-counsel, Jeff Kearney, and me, "Gentlemen, Mrs. Cobb has been present in the courtroom this morning and because of you two men, today may well be the last time I will ever have the opportunity to have lunch with Mrs. Cobb. I will meet you gentlemen at 1:30."

We returned at 1:30 as directed by Judge Cobb and I requested that I be allowed to make a record of what Judge Cobb said to Mr. Kearney and me "off the record" before we broke for lunch. I then stated on the record that Mr. Kearney and I would not accept responsibility for his (Judge Cobb's) indiscretions, as he had suggested off the record, before breaking for lunch. Judge Cobb then told the lawyers to wait in his outer office until we were called back to the courtroom.

We waited in Cobb's outer office for about four hours. He summoned us to the courtroom and announced his decision to remove himself from the case.

Eventually, Judge William Wayne Justice replaced Judge Cobb, and James Wade was sentenced and sent to the penitentiary, he lost everything he owned. His wife moved to a mobile home, and he was legally declared a pauper.

###

My job as a lawyer is to do my best to try to see that my clients get a fair trial. However, the system won't work when a judge conducts himself the way U.S. District Judge Howell Cobb acted against James Wade. Thankfully, a judge like Cobb is in the minority.

Since the verdict, many other lawyers have called, to support me for standing my ground and maintaining my composure under fire. I thanked them and each time I did I also was reminded of my father's words, "No son of mine will ever be a coward".

Howell Cobb was truly every criminal defense attorney's nightmare. To this day, I do not know the basis of his bias, but that doesn't really matter. What does is that my client could not and did not get a fair trial. He was the victim of one of the most toxic and egregious examples of Black Robe Fever I have ever encountered.

The James Wade case was a tragic episode in the annals of American Justice.

CHAPTER 8

ONE EXPLOSION, TWO FORUMS, THREE VICTIMS

A Judge versus Justice

Shortly after midnight on April 17, 1988, Johnnie Lee Davis eyed the darkened interior of Mr. D's Quick Stop, his small convenience store and gasoline station in Temple, Texas. He yawned as he checked to be sure that the front door was locked. Again. It made him mad that he'd had to come back after closing time on a Saturday night, especially since it was his daughter's birthday. Those crazy drunks, he grumbled. Davis looked at his watch. Sunday already! It was less than seven hours before another grueling day at the business he and his wife had purchased only a month earlier.

Johnnie Lee and Sherry Davis had leased and worked at Mr. D's for six years. Now, they owned it. Although his wife came in and helped out a few days each week, Johnnie ran the daily, on-site operations. Sherry's main responsibility was to keep the books straight, which she did at home.

David twisted the knob and pushed against the door to make sure it was secure. He peered through the glass into the darkened store one last time before turning toward his Pontiac that was parked a respectable distance beyond the gasoline pumps. Didn't want to block any customers, he reasoned with a smile.

He started to yawn again when everything around him lit up as if it were noon. Almost instantaneously, he was hurled forward by a broiling and violent force, which seared his back and propelled him across the driveway. His body slammed into one of the gas pumps with such intensity that it uprooted the heavy steel unit that was bolted to a concrete base. Davis, unconscious, tumbled a few more feet across the hard pavement before finally skidding to a stop.

The massive explosion flung debris in all directions. Within seconds, nearby Interstate 35 was littered with the remains of the convenience store, and windows blocks away were shattered. Fortunately for Davis, most of the wood and metal projectiles had passed over him. At their sizes and rate of speed, anyone of them could have killed him.

The night was quiet again. A dog barked forlornly in the distance. Davis regained consciousness, stirred, and struggled to sit up but couldn't. The heavy canopy over the pumps had collapsed, pinning him to the ground. He opened his eyes and attempted to wipe away what felt like warm motor oil, but his fingers wouldn't respond. With the back of his hand, he cleared off some of the sticky substance. In the dim illumination of a nearby streetlight, he noticed that both hands were covered with blood.

Then, the pain hit. He began to moan.

Even though Johnnie Lee was his given name, and many Texas males would have worn the full moniker, he preferred to be called simply, John.

Regardless of the name formality, Davis, 38, was all Texan. Over six feet tall and 185 pounds, he was a pleasant looking guy who was always in motion. His light brown hair was short, and his personality matched his looks: sunny with a generous helping of humor. He'd been born in Bryan, 100 miles northwest of Houston, graduated high school in Cypress, a small town nearer Texas's largest city, and attended the University of Houston for two years. Between high school and college, John spent four years with the Marines, a stint took him to Vietnam for twelve months. John Davis was a doer who found ready friends among his peers. Over some seven and a half years, he managed a Pizza Hut and an Eckerd Drugstore, where he won the praise of his employees.

Sherry Thompson Davis, a nice lady, was also a Texas native. She spent some time in college where she studied business and secretarial administration and had worked as an administrative assistant in Houston for a dozen years.

John and Sherry Davis were married in 1977. Each was divorced. They had two daughters, one of their own and one from Sherry's previous marriage. Their relationship was excellent, with each happily supporting the other regardless of the circumstances. What happened that spring night in 1988 would prove to be the ultimate test for them.

Mr. D's Quick Stop had been a Godsend for the Davises. While it meant a lot of work, seven days a week, they finally had a business of their own. John and Sherry began leasing Mr. D's in 1982. They bought it outright in March of 1988. During that time, their income doubled from what they'd earned in Houston.

Shortly before they purchased Mr. D's, the place had received a needed face-lift that improved its appearance dramatically. It was the newest looking convenience store and service in the vicinity. John and Sherry planned to paint the interior and repair the sidewalks to enhance Mr. D's image even further.

Inside the 3,OOO-square store, the main flooring was linoleum. The rear office was carpeted. The walls were dry wall and paneling. The ceiling was suspended, with dropped fluorescent fixtures. In all, Mr. D's layout was functional, attractive, and the business focus of the Davis' waking hours.

But there were a few headaches. Mr. D's had been burglarized several times, and the Davises had considered installing an alarm system. There was a safe, but it wasn't elaborate, and it was hardly ever used. John hid a little .38 Special there, but, fortunately, he'd never needed it. They never kept much money in the cash register at any time. Vandals had broken in twice, but, they'd done little damage. More serious were the encounters with the owner and patrons of the "Double D," a bar across the parking lot. One evening, the owner himself came over and threatened John.

"He looked Italian and sounded like a terrorist," Davis reported to police.

The troubles with the Double D had increased during the previous year with a change in its clientele to a rougher crowd. Patrons threw bottles against the store, walls spray painted the restroom's outside door. The police stopped by during regular rounds, but they never caught anyone in the act. John had talked with the chief himself on several occasions, but the incidents continued. After one particular scuffle with a drunken patron, John contacted various city officials to ask for their help in cleaning up the area. However, fearing reprisals, he had no intention of participating personally in helping anyone bust the place. Patrons of the Double D regularly parked in the Mr. D lot, and John had frequently complained to the bar's owner. After one such conversation, the owner put a sign on the door advising his customers to park elsewhere, but he took it down a short time later. As John expected, patrons from across the parking lot soon returned to utilize his lot. So he simply had their cars towed away, a solution, which infuriated the owners who bolted into his store to yell at him.

Double D had opened before the city enacted its law limiting the number of parking spaces at commercial establishments, so the Davises couldn't bring force against the bar patrons' many parking abuses. John had considered spreading tacks around the parking lot, but the police warned him not to. The Davis' troubled with the Double D escalated after they bought Mr. D's. Since they had five years invested in their store, they didn't want to run away from the nuisance across the parking lot.

At one point, eight weeks before the explosion, two undercover cops investigated the Double D for drugs and prostitution. The officers stopped by Mr. D's and questioned John about the syringes scattered about his parking lot. He just rolled his eyes and nodded in the direction of the bar. A week before the blast, someone tried to break into the store after John had left. As with previous incidents, he reported it to the police.

Mr. D's usual hours of operation were from 6 a.m. to 9 p.m. Occasionally, for high school games, the Davises would keep the store open as late as midnight. When the problems increased with the unruly patrons of the Double D, John felt compelled to spend more evening time at the store, in order to protect what he and Sherry had worked so hard to establish. If he weren't on duty, and the drunks had a mind to cause trouble, they'd often wander across to Mr. D's where they could display their hostility, unnoticed. Fridays and Saturdays were the worst.

###

Within minutes of the massive explosion, an ambulance steered and skidded around the wreckage of Mr. D's and jerked to a stop. Paramedics dashed toward John's inert and bloody body. He was still alive, but barely conscious. With the help of police officers, they lifted him from beneath the fallen canopy on the debris-strewn parking lot and rushed him to a local hospital where the emergency room physicians did their best. But, good as they were, the doctors had their limits. John's burns were so severe that he was flown to John Sealy Hospital, a renowned burn center in Galveston, where he remained for six weeks.

Davis had suffered third degree burns on his hands, arms, and stomach and second degree burns over ten percent of the rest of his body. He lost his fingers and thumbs and underwent a total of eight surgeries, including skin grafts on his right leg and reconstructive work to give him a thumb and one finger on each hand. There were flash burns on his face, ears, and neck; and cuts on his lips and eyes from flying glass. His hearing was impaired, but miraculously, his eyes weren't affected. It would take more than a year for the experimental medical care of skin grafts and reconstructive surgery to heal his arms.

John didn't remember his first month in the hospital. He had no recollection whatsoever of anything that had happened to him after he turned his head and walked away from Mr. D's that awful night. No memory of the blast, nothing about being thrown across the driveway or how far he went. Nothing.

Some witnesses were certain there had been two distinct explosions. Others maintained that there was only one. Investigators from the Bureau of Alcohol, Tobacco and Firearms and the local *fire* marshal's office were on the scene within hours to attempt to find out. As a matter of "routine procedure," Lone Star Gas Company was called to check the site for leaks and to make sure that any gas to the property was completely turned off, because Mr. D's did not use natural gas, at the time of the explosion, and hadn't had natural gas service for a number of years before this explosion. However, the gas line that once did carry gas service to this location was still in place.

Three days after the explosion, during clean-up activities, the foundation of the building suddenly elevated slightly, then dropped. Afterward, a neighbor smelled natural gas.

John and Sherry had had an ongoing problem with the smell of natural gas at Mr. D's even though they did not use natural gas. They'd often had to open the doors to get rid of the odor, which was usually concentrated in the middle and back of the store. On occasion, it was noticeable throughout the premises. Twice in 1986, once in January and again in December, John had contacted Lone Star Gas to advise that he and his customers had smelled natural gas inside the building. On both occasions, a Lone Star Gas representative visited the store and hurriedly conducted tests with various instruments. The man concluded both times that it was impossible for a natural gas leak to have caused the odor since there was no active hook-up to the building. But that was only half of what the company knew. Lone Star Gas never mentioned that it owned an abandoned pipeline that ran to and under Mr. D's building.

Other business owners in the area had also encountered leaks. Lone Star Gas men did some repair work at a nearby motel one day, but they didn't contact the Davises. In addition, employees of a welding shop just down the road had noticed the smell of natural gas two months before the Mr. D's explosion. About the same time, a man who worked for a grinding company a few blocks away also complained of smelling natural gas. According to some of that business's customers, the ground was once so permeated with the odor that the firm had to shut down welding until the leak was fixed. An auto parts store encountered the same problem.

At the time of the explosion, there was a normal amount of gasoline in the three tanks buried underground at the convenience store. John Davis had not experienced any leaks or other difficulties, other than once-in-a-while breakdowns of the gasoline pumps. They were old, vacuum type, which didn't work very well, in the hot Texas summers. Davis did recall that when the canopies were built over the pumps, workers inserting large supporting posts into the ground thought they'd smelled gas. An evacuation was ordered, but no errant gasoline was found.

At one point, problems developed with the sewer line at Mr. D's. When a company dug it up for testing, a backhoe produced displays of sparks. John wasn't sure if the flashes had come from the company's hitting an underground electrical line or if the men had encountered something in addition to the sewer line. There was a natural gas odor after the incident.

###

One of Mr. D's regular customers was a friendly man named Gary Davis, who wasn't related to John and Sherry. He lived in a nearby motel and frequently came by the store just to visit, many times to talk about buying the couple's old Pontiac. When John had problems with the nightly bar patrons, Gary would rush over with his set of walkie-talkies, and the two men would police the parking lot together. Gary also stayed with John in the store on occasion, for extra protection. All he ever asked for and received were free cokes.

###

When Mr. D's disappeared in an ear-splitting blast, all of John and Sherry's financial matters were in order. They had an excellent relationship with their suppliers, and they had no outstanding personal or business loans at their banks. Other than the mortgage on the store, their only debts were for their home and cars. All of their accounts were current.

John's health was sound. He was under no medical constraints, he was not taking any prescription medication, and he had never abused alcohol or drugs. His doctors later said his good health was a major reason he survived the terrible ordeal.

There was one black mark against John: Some two years earlier, he had been charged and fined for selling liquor to a minor. Other than that, his record was lily white.

The Davises had never been sued by anyone. Their only insurance claim was filed after a tree was struck by lightening.

###

On the day of the explosion, John worked a split shift, from 7 to 10 a.m. and from 6 to 9 p.m. Soon after he arrived in the morning, he discovered that the regular gasoline pump wouldn't operate, but he was so busy with customers that he just hung an "out of order" sign on it. In the evening, when things slowed down, he took off the pump's metal cover and checked the pulleys, which were usually the problem. He had a plastic bucket to catch any spurt of gasoline that might come out during his examination. He couldn't recall if he'd gotten any gasoline on himself in the process. Regardless of his efforts, he couldn't get the pump to operate.

Only the usual customers came in that night. John knew that patrons of the Double D bar were parking behind his store as nine o'clock approached. He tried to call a wrecker to remove the offending vehicles, but he got no response. He knew why. Because of the previous incidents, the wrecker driver was afraid of the Double D crowd, even if a police officer were going to be present while he towed away the cars.

Right at 9 p.m., John closed the store, yet he remained inside to do paperwork and to restock the shelves. No customers came by after he turned off the outside lights.

About a half hour later, Sherry and their youngest daughter arrived. They'd been to a movie to celebrate the girl's birthday and wanted to check on him. He told them he expected trouble from the bar across the street and wouldn't be home until late. After his wife and daughter left, John noticed that one of the restroom lights had burned out, so he left to buy a new one. When he couldn't locate the proper bulb, he drove back to the store. What he saw made him furious. Many more cars had parked behind Mr. D's, and several people were standing around the pay phone on his property, laughing and talking. As he stepped from his car, he was cussing to himself.

"Hey, John, a familiar voice called out. He turned. It was his friend Gary.

"C'mere," John motioned. "Need to throw out the trash ... and the drunks."

He started for the side of the building where the dumpster was located. Too often, an inebriated bar patron snored alongside the metal container. Gary trotted after him.

"Now, don't get all worked up again," John's friend advised with a smile.

John didn't reply. As he turned the comer, he was relieved to see that there weren't any drunks to deal with tonight. Together, the two men tossed several bags into the receptacle.

"Gotta hang around here for a while," John muttered, still angry. "Can't tell what some idiot might do."

"Want me to stay with you?" Gary asked.

"Nah, I'll be alright. I just want them to know I'm here."

His friend shrugged and turned toward his car. John went to the broken gasoline pump. When he saw that no fuel had leaked on the concrete, he walked back to the front door of Mr. D's and peered in for one final check. He knew the electricity to the pumps was turned off, so no one could steal any gasoline. One might get a little residue but no more. Of course, anyone could turn it on if he were to break in and find the key. With everything shut down for the night, John headed for his car, before returning one last time and make sure the front door was locked.

It was weeks before John Davis began recovering his memory. It came back in bits and pieces, but there were gaps in his recollection. He didn't recall, for example, that his friend Gary had come to the hospital to discuss what had happened. He and Gary visited after he was discharged, but many of the things Gary told him were new revelations to him, even though they were matters he should have remembered. John accepted what Gary described because everything Gary said seemed to be right.

In an attempt to piece together why the explosion occurred, John finally remembered that he'd kept extra butane lights and some kerosene in the back room. Sometimes he would store oil and transmission fluid there as well. He wondered if *they* could have exploded.

Many customers of the store, people who had done business with John for over five years, had strong suspicions about the Italian owner of the Double D bar. The speculation was that the bar owner had set this all up and that John wasn't supposed to be at Mr. D's so late. No one was supposed to get hurt, they were certain. They knew about the encounter John had had with the owner, his troubles with the drunks, and his complaints to the police. Yes, the owner must be responsible. John, himself, half believed in their point of view.

In truth, while John knew he hadn't done anything to cause the explosion, he didn't have a clue as to what really happened. Sherry, too, was in the dark. Neither knew if the explosion was intentional or accidental.

###

John and Sherry's insurance agent had arranged a $230,000 policy to cover Mr. D's. Before the explosion, the Davises had routinely gone through the store to estimate the value of its contents. They calculated $30,000, a figure they submitted when they applied for the insurance policy. The insurance paid the loss and John set about getting repairs done so he could re-open.

John Davis was a natural born salesman. At least he had most of the attributes. He always wanted to make a statement about something, and then sell that statement to anyone who would listen. That was one of the problems Vic Feazell and I had with him. When I read the sworn statement he gave to the insurance company just after the explosion, I couldn't believe my eyes. Since many people knew about his troubles with the Double D, and had concluded that the owner or someone else connected with the bar had torched his store, John apparently didn't want to let them down. It sounded like a good story, so John picked up on the theory and tried to sell the insurance company on it. Fortunately, not too long afterwards, when Mr. D's had been rebuilt and was again open for business, John was introduced to a new possibility. One day someone said to him, "Don't you remember that, from time to time, you'd smell natural gas in your building?" John thought about it for a second. "Hey, you're right." "Well, why don't you go down to city hall and look at the old records dealing with Lone Star Gas to see if there are any pipelines in the vicinity?"

John went to the records department. He wasn't prepared for the reception he received.

"No!"

"Beg your pardon?"

"You can't see those records."

Something wasn't right. Why would a resident be denied access to public records? It was all very suspicious.

As soon as he left city hall, John started developing what he considered to be evidence of a natural gas problem. He remembered and wrote down the various occasions when he'd had the situation at Mr. D's, as well as the incidents he knew his neighbors had had. When he'd compiled his list, he tried to hire a local lawyer. Curiously, he faced another chilly reception. Nobody in town would take his case. Finally, someone referred him to Vic Feazell, who still lived in Waco. John was elated when Vic quickly agreed to represent him, but he faced one more obstacle: a threatened arson charge.

The district attorney informed Feazell that if he filed a lawsuit on John's behalf, John would be indicted for arson. Vic's client had better "let sleeping dogs lie." Regardless of the threat, the suit was filed. Shortly before the trial, I joined the case.

John's first deposition, which was taken before he did his research and hired Vic Feazell, advanced the notion that the Double D crowd was probably responsible for the explosion, created a lot of trouble for us. His second one advanced a new theory. When I read the two depositions, I said, "John, we've got a real problem. There are all kinds of ways they can cut you up on the stand, because you've said so many inconsistent things. You have two objectives ... and only two. First, when you get off the stand, I want the jury to like you. Second, when you're asked whether or not you torched your own building, I want you to have conviction when you tell the folks you didn't. Don't try to sell anything. Just answer the questions. Your job is to simply tell 'em, not sell 'em."

The lawsuit was styled, <u>Johnnie Lee Davis and Sherry Davis v. Lone Star Gas Co.</u>, a division of Enserch Corporation. Trial was set for Bell County District Court in Belton, Texas. On the courthouse records, it was referred to simply as Case No. 128,597-C.

Vic Feazell and I had two expert witnesses: Dr. Gerald Hurst from Austin and Ken Gibson from Arlington, Texas. Attorneys for Lone Star Gas were Dustin Fillmore of Ft. Worth, Bob Burleson of Temple, Texas, and Max Hendrick with Enserch Corporation.

While we were picking the jury we learned that Bob Burleson, a local lawyer who had been hired by Lone Star Gas about a month before the trial, was the former law partner of Judge Pemberton who was going to hear our case. Vic Feazell was told by someone in the court clerk's office that we were in for a really tough ride because Pemberton would do anything Burleson wanted him to do. That little revealing statement opened our eyes. We had to be prepared for a bad situation again.

What should have happened, of course, is that the judge, immediately upon Burleson being hired, should have notified us of this previous connection. But he didn't. It would prove to be another instance of Black Robe Fever.

During Burleson's voir dire, we learned that Judge Pemberton and Bob Burleson had remained close personal friends over the years. They traveled and hunted together. It was a little late then to do anything about this cozy agreement, because we wanted to go to trial. However, having that information enabled me to develop a strategy that I thought might help us. A couple of days later, the judge and the attorneys, two or three of us, were standing around talking. Something came up about lawyers writing books, and I told Pemberton that I was doing just that.

"Oh, really?" He looked wary.

"Yes, indeed," I replied with a grin.

The judge squinted at me. "What's it about?"

I was so glad he asked.

"It's a book about how to deal with judges who, as I put it, get out of line in the courtroom. It's for the public, because the stories are interesting, but it's particularly for young lawyers who don't know how to deal with a situation when a judge decides to get out of line in the courtroom."

After a moment's reflection, Pemberton said, "Well, that's interesting. I'd like to have a copy."

"Oh, yes," I promised. "I'll get you one as soon as it's published."

A few days later, one of our key expert witnesses was on the stand, and Burleson was cross-examining him. Without any objection from Burleson or anyone else, the judge laid into our expert witness, who was doing a great job and obviously damaging the defense's position, telling him to quit playing games with the lawyer and that he could answer Burleson's questions with a simple "yes" or "no." More than anything, what bothered me was Pemberton's tone of voice, I asked for permission to approach the bench. I wanted to make a record. The judge waved us forward.

"Your honor, from our side of the courtroom the tone of voice you just used in saying the things that you said to Mr. Gibson, (our expert), showed, in our opinion, anger, hostility, and possibly prejudice. At this point I'm not prepared to accuse you of

trying to throw this case for your former law partner, but I am
sufficiently concerned that in the future if you feel like you need to
say something to one of our witnesses, particularly in the tone of
voice that you just used a few minutes ago, it's our request that it
be done out of the presence of the jury, because, judge, unless you
convince me otherwise, I'm still going to assume that you aren't
attempting to prejudice this jury against our side of the case. I
hope I'm correct in my assumption, and I hope there's no reason
for me to think otherwise from here on." From that point,
Pemberton was a perfect jurist. One of his staff members caught
me in the hall and said, "We heard what you said to Judge
Pemberton. We love it!" We came to learn that he wasn't
particularly liked by his staff, and certainly not respected.

During the course of the trial, Lone Star Gas produced
witnesses who revealed that both the ATF and the local fire
marshal had attempted, on at least five separate occasions, to try
and get the district attorney to file arson charges against John
Davis. To the authorities, the Mr. D's explosion was a classic
arson case. Needless to say, no settlement offers were made to us.

We introduced testimony that on the day after the explosion
Lone Star Gas was on the scene digging and finding gas leaks in
the vicinity. Even though the company testified that they really
weren't gas leaks, one of its own witnesses admitted that he had
seen Lone Star Gas personnel discover a leak at the motel across
the street from the Davis' store.

Our position was firm: the explosion and fire had occurred
because Mr. D's was on the highest peak in the area, there was an
abandoned Lone Star Gas line directly under the store, natural gas
had been allowed to migrate into the old line, many resulting leaks
had been discovered over time and had been set off that night by a
spark from an ice maker or similar electrical device. It was open
and shut, as far as we were concerned. The jury agreed and
awarded the Davises $11,815,000 in actual damages and $10
million in punitive damages.

The defendants immediately filed a motion for a new trial or,
in the alternative, a reduction in the amount awarded. At the
hearing on this motion, I was prepared for the worst. I'd heard
stories about the judge, how one never knew what he was going to

do, and that he'd likely do anything. When a newly hired appellate lawyer from Houston made his argument on behalf of Lone Star Gas, it was that the verdict should be reduced, at the very least. He said, "There's no way this case is worth more than $1 million - maybe $3 million, tops. I've been in this business a lot of years, and, judge, if you don't give us a new trial, you should at least reduce it."

Pemberton asked him, "Well, do you agree that if I make a decision to reduce it that I've got to do one, two, and three things?" He enumerated several procedural steps.

The lawyer nodded. "Yes, I agree with that."

The judge looked around the room. "Does anyone else have anything to say before I make a decision?"

I can't remember exactly what I said, but the gist of it was, "Yeah, judge, I'd like to say a few things. You know, I'm always appalled at the ability of someone to do what this young lawyer over here from Houston just did for us. He seems to think he's capable of coming in here after the fact, and telling all of us what this case is worth, even though we spent three weeks in front of a jury asking them what it was worth. And interestingly enough, they had the opportunity to hear the facts, and I would say all of them were reasonably intelligent, and some of them highly educated. Matter of fact, there were five college professors on the jury since the small town of Belton, Texas, with a population of less that 10,000, was the home of Mary Hardin Baylor University. They heard the facts, and, moreover, they heard Mr. and Mrs. Davis tell what they have had to suffer and what they're still suffering, as well as what they will have to suffer for the rest of their lives because of that explosion."

"Maybe what this young lawyer needs to do is hear some of that. Maybe we ought to let him go back into the courtroom for a few minutes and visit with Mr. and Mrs. Davis and see how confident he is then in his ability to come in here and tell us what this lawsuit's worth. So it disturbs me greatly that you would even imply or indicate that you're considering a reduction on this verdict based on what this newcomer has to say.

"And I want to add another factor, and that's this: our judicial system is under attack today, and some of it may be deserved, because it's a big concern to the public, and it's equally of concern to me, as to what a person can do with one stroke of the pen to undo what a jury has done. We had twelve smart people who heard the evidence, and they told us what this case is worth. But now you can take your pen and literally destroy what those jurors have done. We know they were impartial because we voir-dired them on it. They didn't have any interest one way or the other, yet when one person who might be prejudiced can undo what those people have done, that's why we're having so much criticism of our system today, and legitimately so, because you never know where prejudices may be coming from."

I stared at Judge Pemberton.

"You've already taken one whack at this verdict, and you're saying that you did it because of a technical matter, and I can understand that there are times, technical reasons, for a judge to have to do some things, so I'm not going to debate that issue with you. It's water under the bridge as far as what we're here to do today.

"But what I would recommend to you is not only to preserve the integrity of our system but also to sign the order just as it remains, and let this little couple go home and get a good night's rest for the first time in a long time."

What I said had to be said. I know that few lawyers ever talk to a judge the way I did, but it was my responsibility to do so on behalf of my clients. Seconds later, the judge agreed and let the judgment stand.

Judge Pemberton did take away our punitive damage award of $10 million, which didn't surprise us nor did it bother us as we were well pleased with the $12 million that remained. After all, we had offered to settle for far less and did, in fact settle the case while it was on appeal for a small reduction of the judgment for actual damages rendered by the jury. Believe me, Vic and I were satisfied and our client was ecstatic.

A final note on Judge Pemberton. Vic Feazell personally found a local lawyer who he helped greatly with funds, to run against Pemberton at his next reelection. Vic's candidate defeated Pemberton. This was in 1994.

One thing I'll never forget happened on the day we were going to court to make our closing argument. The Davis' young daughter looked at her mother and asked, "When all of this is over, do you think we'll have enough money so I can get a new pair of designer jeans?" Thankfully, in spite of several bouts of Black Robe Fever, John and Sherry were able to grant their little girl's wish.

CHAPTER 9

A SPREADING EPIDEMIC

The Abuses Abound

"Black robe fever" doesn't discriminate. It exists in Federal, state, and local courtrooms across America. No jurisdiction is immune from the arrogant excesses of judges out of control, and, at one time or another, virtually every trial attorney will confront this sad abuse of power. What he or she does about it can mean the difference between effective representation of the client and the surrender of that client to the worst our system has to offer.

A judge may attempt to intimidate and influence every minute of the legal proceeding, or he may focus solely on one area of the trial. In either instance, justice suffers. Here are some condensed versions of other encounters I've had in the courtroom with Black Robe Fever judges.

###

I remember one case I had in the state district court in Dallas. The judge, whom I'll refer to as Bentley, called the attorneys in on the Friday before the trial was to start. As soon as we assembled in his chambers, he said he wanted to make sure we understood what his rules were, because we were going to follow them or else.

"Fifteen minutes for voir dire, fifteen minutes for your opening statement, and twenty minutes for closing argument." Bentley sat forward in his elevated leather chair, staring down at each of us in turn. From his pursed-lips expression, I knew he was daring any one of us to challenge his unbelievably restrictive and ruthless boundaries that he had set for us. Well, the "challenge" was just too much for me to not accept, so when Judge Bentley asked if there were any questions, I just couldn't resist.

I smiled. "No questions your honor, but I do have some comments."

He frowned.

"And I'd like to make them on the record," I added quickly, before he could respond. I continued. 'Judge, I know this case far better than you will ever know it, and I can tell you that there's absolutely no way I can do justice to a voir dire or an opening statement in fifteen minutes. The purpose of the opening statement, after all, is to give an overview of the case, and there's no way I can do that in this case in fifteen minutes."

"I would like to let you know that I represent some people who are a part of a very special class. They're called taxpayers. And, judge, they are the very ones who paid to have the courtroom built, and they pay your salary, as well as that of your staff. And the reason they do, judge, is so that in the event they have a legal problem they are in hopes that they can come to the courthouse and get a fair trial, which you, by the way, are denying them."

Judge Bentley held up his hand. "Mr. Richardson, I've had lawyers come in before who aren't real pleased with my rules, but they find out that things work out all right."

I shook my head. "Judge, don't be mistaken into believing that the lawyers feel your rules are fair, because if they tell you that then they are lying to me. I've talked to enough lawyers around town to know that they feel you're not fair in the way you run your courtroom."

The judge pondered for a few seconds.

"All right, Mr. Richardson," he replied, "I'll make an exception. Instead of fifteen minutes for your voir dire and fifteen for your opening statement, I'll give you twenty."

He grimaced as if he had made a major concession, then he grinned. "For each of them."

I wanted to laugh, but I restrained myself.

"Now, judge," I said, "you might want to reconsider that because, knowing that you are a conservative Republican, you might get to thinking about it over the weekend and feel like you'd become a complete liberal."

I knew that he had once run for attorney general on the Republican ticket and was considered very conservative. At that point he chuckled and then dismissed us. As we filed out of his chambers, I hoped I'd made an impact.

###

I had an encounter with another district judge in Dallas. This man had been nominated to the Federal bench, but, fortunately, Congress didn't confirm him.

My client was a man who, I believe, was gravely wronged by a law firm. The firm had churned his case and, in my opinion, grossly over billed him. In one case, the man had been sued for $217,000. By the time he realized what was going on, he'd paid the law firm over $400,000 in attorneys fees, and there still was no end in sight. My client owned a large company and was quite well off, and he hadn't kept tabs on the lawyers' shenanigans. When he came to me for help, I was appalled. The more I learned, the madder I got. We sued the law firm for malpractice.

Once we came before the judge, he threw the case out. Not only that, when I asked for a hearing on the matter, he set one for Friday afternoon, when he denied our motion. The reason he scheduled the hearing when he did was obvious. His court reporter wouldn't be available. He didn't want a record made of his conduct, or else the lay person would have no clue that his "court reporter" was off on Friday afternoons unless they were in trial. No one was there to make a record.

This case is now on appeal, and I am hopeful we'll get a reversal. I noticed recently in the Texas Lawyer magazine that there was an angry letter to the editor by a lawyer who felt that this judge hadn't been treated fairly by Congress in not confirming him. Interestingly, the writer of the letter was one of the attorneys in the law firm we'd sued.

The story of Janet Anniboli looked like a hopeless cause when I took her case a few years ago. Janet had pleaded guilty to a criminal charge before she hired me. My job was to withdraw that plea, something that is far easier to ask for than to accomplish. Her guilty plea had been entered in federal court in Beaumont, Texas.

Janet Anniboli told me that she had pleaded guilty because her lawyer was not prepared to defend her case the day they appeared in court to begin her trial. So, he pressured her into guilty plea. Almost in tears, she said that since her lawyer wasn't prepared to go to trial, the man put all kinds of pressure on her. He told her she was going to be found guilty and was going to get years in the penitentiary. All this even though she had paid him a handsome fee to represent her, and, all along, had led her to believe that she had little to be concerned about.

I might add that her story was not all that difficult for me to believe, because, sadly, I've seen it happen too often. Lawyers take fees, don't get ready to try a case, and then tell their clients all the reasons why they're going to lose so they might as well throw in the towel. Such actions are a blight on the legal profession.

In any event, Janet was not only intimidated by her lawyer to enter a guilty plea, her lawyer admonished her that when the judge asked questions she had to state that her plea was of her own free will. That's why it's so difficult to get a judge to allow someone to withdraw a guilty plea. As long as it's the defendant's decision (after all, who better would know if he or she were innocent?), the plea stands. Almost everyone can become remorseful later. But that doesn't matter if the plea were entered without coercion.

I believed Janet's story. A woman friend of hers confirmed it. She told me that the two of them had gone to the lawyer's office on two or three occasions but that the attorney had passed the word that he was too busy to see them. The woman added that Janet had tried and failed to get in touch with her lawyer for a week or so immediately preceding the trial date. In short, he had not spent any time with his client in order to get ready for trial. I agreed to take her case.

I knew the odds of winning were slim to none. I was hoping for slim, at best. When I went to Beaumont to petition for the withdrawal of Janet's guilty plea, I didn't have a canned speech in mind. It came to me as I was watching and listening to what was happening in the courtroom that day.

What I saw the court place its attention on was, first, the fact that this lady had pleaded guilty after he had gone through all the requisite questions, and, second, he made a big point that it was time-consuming and costly for the Federal court to grant such a request. When I stood to speak, I was ready.

"Judge," I began. "As I've sat here today and listened, I've largely determined that the court has two major concerns. One is the fact that this lady has pleaded guilty and that she said it was of her own free will and volition, and I want to address that. And, secondly, the fact that the court is concerned about the time and cost factor that will be involved with the U.S. Attorney's office and the court in the trying of this case. I want to tell you that I believe that if the court places any degree of reliability on the testimony given during this hearing, the court has to acknowledge that there does seem to be a ring of truth to the testimony of Mrs. Anniboli and her friend that her lawyer did not get prepared for trial, that her lawyer did, in fact, intimidate her into entering her plea of guilty by telling her she was going to lose and by telling her what was going to happen when she lost in a trial versus the plea negotiation that was going on."

There wasn't a sound in the courtroom. I think most spectators thought they were witnessing someone attempting a hurdle rivaling Evel Knevel' s jump over the Grand Canyon.

"And judge," I went on, "I have to tell you that my real concern is that the court is focusing on the cost, the time, and the trouble. As I stand here today, I can think back to many instances of my training as a lawyer when I was told, and it was emphasized time and time again, that our system was one of justice. I have to ask myself one question: If that's the case, where does the discussion of cost come into that formula? How can cost be a factor if our system is really about justice? I heard Mrs. Anniboli, under oath tell you her reasoning, and I believe it's true, and I think that even this court believes it's true, so we're boiling it down largely to one thing, and that's the cost factor."

I held out my hands to show a balancing. "Judge, if you allow the cost factor and the time factor to this court and the U.S. Attorney's office to have any significance whatsoever in your decision on this matter, then I say that the scales of justice are tarnished. They have no meaning. But, judge, I believe that our scales of justice do have meaning. And I believe today that even you will come to realize that more important than time, more important than money, more important than anything else in the life of this lady is for her to know that our court system does in fact give her an opportunity for justice. There's only one way that can happen, Judge, and that's for you to allow this woman to tell her story to a jury and let that jury make the decision as to whether she's guilty or innocent."

Those in the courtroom stirred as I built my case. I took it as a good sign.

"If you deny her that right, let's no longer speak of justice. Let's speak of cost. Let's speak of practicality. Let's speak of time, but let's never again talk about justice, because it's only a theory and has no meaning. Thank you very much, Your Honor."

For what seemed like thirty minutes, which was no more than two or three, one could hear a pin drop. Finally, the judge said he needed to take a thirty-minute recess.

Before I began my statement, I knew that few had any doubts about the outcome: the judge was going to summarily overrule our motion to withdraw Janet's plea. But when I finished and the judge exited the courtroom, many of those in the gallery, people in attendance in the courtroom on other legal matters came up to me. They enthusiastically expressed their belief that, even though rarely ever granted, they did believe the judge would grant our motion.

"There's no question what he's going to do," one man whispered. "He has no alternative. He'll allow you to withdraw your plea." I hoped he was right.

A half-hour later, the judge came back into the courtroom and sat down. In a measured tone, he granted our motion. It was such a unique event in Federal court that the statewide Texas Lawyer magazine wrote a major article about it. Such a reversal does happen in state courts, but I don't know if I had ever heard of it happening before in the Federal system.

A few years ago, there was a lawsuit against a bank and an individual in Oklahoma City that demonstrated again a local judge's favoritism toward the power structure. I was trying the case for an attorney named Vic Grider. At the end of our case-in-chief, the judge made a ruling to let the bank off the hook. He didn't give much reasoning for his decision, so Grider (who was handling the motions and the technical, legal part of the trial), stood up and asked the judge if he would state for the record the reasoning for his ruling. With a frown, the judge told my associate, Mr. Grider, that he didn't have time to spend the rest of the afternoon trying to help him understand his ruling, after which he turned to the bailiff and told him to bring in the jury. He turned to the other side and told them to call their next witness.

I immediately stood up. "Your honor, I'd like to make my own record before we call for the jury, and I'd like to say this. It is my understanding that what's really important today is justice for this lady, Mrs. Barbara Dew. Judge, I know you're busy, but so is everyone in the courtroom, but that's not the issue. It is my understanding that in our profession, the issue is justice. And judge, the only just thing for you to do is for you to state your reasons for your ruling and make a record so if we want to appeal, we'll have a proper basis on which to do it. In all honesty, judge, if it takes you the rest of the day to do that which is fair for Mrs. Dew, that's exactly what we expect you to do and that's exactly what we want you to do."

As soon as I sat down, the judge looked at me, nodded, then took the time to tell us, on the record, why his reasons were what they were. Had I not stood up and made my point, this client would not have received fair treatment under our system of justice. It's because I, as a lawyer, was willing to take the risk of being attacked by a court in order to see to it that justice was done on her behalf that we got what was needed for an appeal, and by the way, the ruling dismissing the bank was appealed. The judge's ruling was reversed, and the case was later tried in another court and the plaintiff got a jury verdict in excess of $200,000. This never could have happened had the Judge not been forced to put the reasons for his ruling for dismissing the case against the bank on the record.

In one case against a powerful banker in a town several hundred miles away, I loaded my car with clothes and drove seven or eight hours. My expert witness and I cleared our calendars for the two weeks we anticipated the trial would take. However, that was not to be. The judge immediately granted a continuance at the request of the banker's attorneys. This happened not once but three times! Such dilatory actions were obviously taken to help the local defendant, but, more significantly, they were another example of the abuse of our system of justice by the one individual upon whom we should be able to rely for impartiality ... the judge.

On the fourth occasion that I drove to Palestine, Texas with enough clothes for a week-long trial, we got to go to trial. We won and got a verdict in excess of $500,000.00

When John Cathey, an old client from Waco, Texas called, I heard it in his voice. He was stressed and without hope. He told his story. John had been in commercial real estate development for few years with Larry Meyer. I, of course, knew Larry Meyer, the son of a well-known Waco family. His father was Paul Meyer, a motivational guru and founder of Success Motivation. I had once owned a Success Motivation franchise, had known Paul for years, and had even met and played golf with Larry. More than an old client, John was a friend as well. I had to help him.

To help in John's case, I worked with a Waco law firm headed up by Dale Williams, who has become one of my closest friends. Waco had grown to almost 250,000, but the Meyer family was so well known and held such political strength there that we found it necessary to bring a judge in from outside of Waco to handle the trial. Little did that help.

Things got so heated one morning in the courtroom that as I walked past a juror seated on a bench in the hallway on my way back from lunch, he said to me, "Go get'em, Tiger". He obviously referred to an exchange between the judge and me that morning.

It was a six-week and some day trial. Reported to have been the longest in the County's history, two days longer than the Feazell trial. We won and the jury gave us all that we asked, in excess of $3M. Unfortunately, that didn't' end the story.

The defense filed motions to have the verdict set aside, something extremely rare. Jurors learned of the motion the defense had filed. After all, it was big news because of who the Meyer family was and the size of the verdict. To our surprise, when we showed up in court to argue the motion, several jurors were in the courtroom. They, too, wanted to see what would happen.

Judge Meier (different spelling from the defendant in the case), listened to arguments, as if he truly was struggling with what to do. It was all show. He obviously knew what he was going to do before he came to the courtroom. And, he did just what the defendants wanted. He dismissed the case. He set the verdict aside, to our great surprise. We were, however, confident, as we knew that the appellate court would correct his obvious misdeed. A court that was located right there in Waco, in the same courthouse as the courtroom where we tried the case.

We filed briefs. The law was on our side: nothing to worry about. Also, one of the three appellate judges on the court to hear the appeal was a very close friend to Mr. Williams, the local lawyer on the case. They attended the same Church and had sung together in a gospel quartet for years. We were really only concerned about one of the three judges, but two were all we needed.

The call came from Dale Williams, "Gary, you won't believe this, but the appellate court upheld Judge Meier's ruling to dismiss our verdict." To say we were 'shocked' doesn't come close. We had seen no way anyone could do this! I hadn't heard the most shocking part. Dale continued, "Gary, you're not going to believe this, but 'my friend' wrote the opinion against us, and the judge we were concerned about wrote a strong opinion *for* us. But the vote was 2-1 against us and, 'my friend' did it to us."

Within days of the opinion's release by the appellate court, Dale's friend resigned from the court, and went to work at a large law firm in Waco. Obviously by happenstance I am sure, it was the same law firm where the Meyers family had been clients for years.

I sometimes wonder how some people sleep at night. But then again, I see, as I know you do, all the advertisements for sleeping pills and various other sleeping aids. But here, a few of the system's rotten apples took a $3Million plus verdict from my friend, John Cathey. Maybe another example of how the rich got richer and the poor got poorer. As I say from time to time, if I was going to do something to a person like this, I would as soon rob a bank. To me, the abuse that occasionally takes place in our legal system is a worse type of corruption than those who rob banks. It is an abuse of trust that the people have placed in them. How can it get any worse?

###

The cases I share with you in this book are, as I have already emphasized, true and exceptions to the general rule. From over 200 courtroom trials, I could share many wonderful courtroom experiences and many honorable judges. Thankfully, the "fever" that I have written about in this book has not infected so many of them. And this book's purpose is not to cause alarm at our judiciary system. It is more to educate the public on insisting that their lawyer represent them fully, and more to encourage trial lawyers to stand up for their clients when they encounter a "bad apple" in the system. The gain far outweighs the loss. As I say so often to lawyers, be a warrior for your client, they are entitled to it.

###

Just as this book was going to publication I encountered a judge with Black Robe Fever. Interesting enough, I have filed, within the past 30 days a judiciary complaint against a State Court Judge here in Oklahoma. This is only the 2nd time in my 36 year legal career that I have done so. The first, as you know, was Judge Carter and when I was in my first year as a practicing attorney.

This judge serves in one of the outlying counties and abused a couple of the lawyers in our law firm (The Richardson Law Firm, Tulsa, Oklahoma). In talking to some lawyers in and around the County where this judge sits on the bench, I learned of some, even to me, fairly unbelievable stories. I am not free to share with you either who the judge is, or the stories, as the complaint that I filed is still pending and it would be a violation for me to do so.

CHAPTER 10

BREAKING THE FEVER

A Prescription for Relief

More than two hundred years ago, Thomas Jefferson proclaimed, "The execution of the laws is more important than the making of them."

I built my practice on that simple yet compelling statement, and that same statement compelled me to write this book. Too often, when a man or woman puts on the robe that is the ultimate symbol of justice, a dark side of his or her personality hides beneath it. In those instances we are challenged to deal with an insidious wrong that seriously threatens to damage our precious system of justice. A judge infected with Black Robe Fever becomes an aberrant maverick, and an undeniable threat to Jefferson's elegant principle.

I hope this book will educate and inspire. When a problem comes, regardless of what it is or how large it is, I hope that the defender of justice will address that problem, even when it's unpopular to do so, even when his or her safety is threatened with a fine or contempt of court citation.

It is not easy to write about this subject. As an attorney, it grieves me that Black Robe Fever causes the problems that it does. It is paramount that people throughout our society begin to realize what has happened to our system of justice in the rare instances of Black Robe Fever judges, and become motivated to make the necessary changes to get back to the Constitutional principles of Thomas Jefferson and the other founders of our great nation. This will happen with more effective handling of the abusive judges in the Judiciary Committees that oversee them.

One of the temptations in our daily lives is "to count the costs." It actually sounds like the right thing to do. However, when we decide what is right or wrong based on the perceived price, the incorrect path can be chosen — and frequently is. Throughout the years, in my role as an advocate in the courtroom, I've tried never

168

to count the costs I might have to pay personally when I see a job that needs to be done in order to seek justice for a client.

I guess I was born to be a lawyer. Even as a young boy I knew I wanted to do something that would make a difference in my life and in the lives of others. For as long as I can remember I've defended the underdog, the "little guy," who seems to have the odds stacked against him, yet the people in the stands are most often pulling for. And this is the key to dealing with a Judge that has Black Robe Fever. If you, the lawyer, can help the jury see what the Judge is doing to your underdog, you will most often get the support of that jury.

My father received only a third-grade education, and was the hardest-working man I've ever known. As a sharecropper, he sometimes had to hold down three jobs to provide the necessities of life for my mother, my twin sister, and me. Often, he'd water cotton all night, and then sell cars the entire next day ... for a week at a time. I'm sure he caught some sleep on the bank of a water ditch, but his head never touched a pillow. Dad always said his ambition in life was to have been a judge. I never asked him why, but knowing him, and his love for people, I imagine he considered it to be an important and as much of a respected profession as I do.

The early' 50s presented tough financial times for my family, and I didn't get to spend as much time with Dad as I would have liked because he was always working to fulfill his aspiration for me to get a college education. He talked about it all the time and said to me of his hard work, "I'm doing this for you, son."

People say we are in large measure the product of our environment. I know a lot of what I am today is because of my religious upbringing as well, and I am so thankful for that.

I did go to college and three years after graduation from college, decided to attend law school part time. By this time I was married and had two sons, and a job as a full time insurance adjustor.

I guess I became an attorney, in part, to pay tribute to what my Dad so greatly admired and desired. In 1972 I graduated from law school, still adhering to the principles I'd learned from my parents and with total faith in our judicial system. My expectations, just like those of most new law school graduates, were that justice would always be served-our judges would make certain of it. I was bright-eyed and bushy-tailed, as they say, ready and eager to practice law. I thought that if I represented my clients fairly and honestly, we would be accorded equal treatment in return.

Prior to graduation from law school, the only time I had been in a courtroom was as an insurance adjuster. I'd never before been involved in a courtroom proceeding, observed the jury selection process, or even watched a trial on television or in the movies. Since I worked full-time, I didn't have the luxury of being able to do such things. I barely had time to go to law school and get ready for class.

I finished law school having been taught nothing about lawyer's rights in the courtroom or how to work with judges. This fact seems even more incredible to me today than it did thirty-five plus years ago. The topics were simply never discussed. And, shockingly, little has changed. The only areas of law school that might deal with these important matters are moot during court and trial court competition. Both courses comprise only a very small portion of a law student's education, and merely a handful of students participate in the latter. In addition, there are no classes whatsoever which teach how to deal with judges who "get out of line" in the courtroom. And as far as I know, there is no definitive textbook anywhere that deals with proper ways to deal with bad judges.

I didn't realize the importance of these issues until I began practicing law and saw how fearful most lawyers are of judges infected with Black Robe Fever. Most lawyers do not know what their recourse is if a judge shows prejudice and is unfair to their client. Since law schools continue to produce attorneys who are unprepared for a judge who wants to control, far too often, the outcome of a case. The problem can only get worse.

Just how is our legal system supposed to work? In other words, what is real justice? Under our system, individuals have the right to select a lawyer to represent them in various legal matters and to go into a court of law on their behalf, if that becomes necessary. Every one of us has the right to have our case heard. As citizens, we pay tax dollars for the right to have a forum available to us if we choose to litigate our differences of opinion, just as we pay for highways, the protection of police, and other necessary public services.

Some lawyers obviously have better trial skills than others, but people have the right to hire whomever they choose. In a lawsuit, justice does not occur until both sides have lawyers who give total effort to their clients' cases without the improper interference of a third party, who too often can be the judge. If one lawyer is outperforming the other, some judges seem to feel they are supposed to step in and balance the scales. They do not have such a right, and such intervention is not justice. It's the opposite.

A judge's role is much like that of a referee in a ball game. It is to maintain order in the courtroom so that a fair trial results within the confines of the rules and guidelines.

How do attorneys and clients know what their rights are when a judge oversteps his boundaries? Sadly, most attorneys can't say, and only a very small percentage of clients have a hint.

Each state has its own judicial canons and restrictions on judges, but, in the real world, it's usually up to each judge to exercise his or her own discretions. Because of this latitude, it's no wonder things are in such a mess and certain judges get away with obvious prejudice. Judges are probably less accountable and have more immunity from being punished for their misdeeds than professionals in any other field. This is an extremely dangerous situation, particularly as judges deal with our basic and precious rights as citizens of the United States.

To me, it is paramount, if a lawyer plans to prepare him/herself to take on a judge, if need be, that it be done with style. I can't say how many times over the years that it has been suggested that, "Yes, Gary, you can get by with that." They cite my age, my gray hair, that I've been a US Attorney, and on and on. But I confronted judges as a young assistant DA and as a then-black-headed lawyer, long before I became a private attorney.

What to me are the key factors?

First and foremost, you must have a passion in your belly for justice, in order to be willing to take the risks involved with representing your client fully with a judge that has Black Robe Fever

That being said, the key elements, as I see them are:

1. Always show respect to the Judge, especially when in front of the jury. Let the judge show his or her a_ _, but always be professional, always.

2. Never, never, never argue with the Judge. You typically won't win, even with those who aren't affected with Black Robe Fever.

3. Always look the Judge in the eyes. Always.

4. Again, always respect, but never cower. This only spurs a judge with Black Robe Fever even more.

5. Make records. Make records. Make records. This is an excellent method to get said what you want to say and all you are doing is making a record, which you are entitled to do.

6. Be incredibly honest. Always. Not doing so keeps you in fear of being found out and takes away your "will" to never cower.

7. In making records, be explicit about the judge's conduct, but do it with professionalism and factually. State the facts.

8. Remember this. Your objectives are to win over the jury, to have a good record for appeal purposes, to be professional and to never cower.

What can a lawyer, client, or citizen do if a judge has been unfair in a trial? Currently, in the legal profession the standard answer is, one can appeal. But all across the country we find outrageous conduct on the part of judges that are never challenged. If a particular action is appealed, judgment lies in the hands of that judge's peers. It would be far better if a jury of twelve ordinary people examined the case. I assure you there would be a different outcome in many, if not most, of the questionable actions.

When something is appealed, we usually have to wait until the higher court decides before we can ask that a judge be disqualified. And that can take three to five years! The damage has been done, and the matter is settled. Of course, if the judge's behavior was particularly egregious, the party might be granted a new trial, but again, a lot of time has passed, and the chances of righting a wrong at such a late date are close to nil.

Then, I remember a comment I made to Judge Mormino in the Steele case: "You know my clients can't afford an appeal," and he did know that they couldn't. This, of course, kept the higher judges from seeing how he conducted himself during the trial.

We obviously don't live in a perfect world, but when we talk of representing a client, in many cases being paid an hourly rate, we carry a great responsibility and I do hope that one day I will look back on my career as a lawyer and know that I gave it my very best. I gave my clients the best that I had. Then I will lay my head on my pillow and rest in peace.

Also, as you see from reading these cases that I shared, the judge wasn't influenced by what was happening in the courtroom, but rather who the parties were in the courtroom. If you don't typically represent clients that cause you to go up against powerful opponents, you most likely will never experience what you have read about in this book.

Some lawyers have a mistaken belief that it's about being "nice" to the judge. In the type of cases I have shared here, being nice would have been a worse situation for my clients. Most probably, the cases would never have been won.

THE KEY: NEVER FIND YOURSELF 'JUSTIFYING' WHY YOU DON'T STAND UP FOR YOUR CLIENTS. NEVER.

HAPPY LAWYERING.
IT'S A GREAT PROFESSION.
HONOR THE PROFESSION.

WE, AS TRIAL LAWYERS,
CAN NEVER GIVE UP
AND
CAN NEVER GIVE IN TO
BLACK ROBE FEVER.